**Rosalind K Marshall**

Edinburgh
The Trustees of the National Galleries of Scotland
1979

# Women in Scotland 1660-1780

# Contents

# Introduction

ost of the historical figures represented in a portrait gallery are men—the soldiers, statesmen and lawyers who shaped a nation's past. Yet the part played by women should not be underestimated, for documentary evidence suggests that their range of activities was far wider than is often supposed. This booklet is designed to give a glimpse of the lives of Scotswomen of the period 1660–1780 through their portraits, their letters and brief accounts of their careers. As always, there is a preponderance of information about the aristocracy, simply because the pictures and papers of the noble families have been preserved. Whenever possible, however, material relating to other sections of society has been included. It should also be noted that there is no attempt to discuss here one of a woman's principal preoccupations, the bearing and rearing of her children. This was the theme of the Scottish National Portrait Gallery's 1976 exhibition and reference may be made to its catalogue, *Childhood in Seventeenth Century Scotland*, by the present author.

In preparing *Women in Scotland 1660–1780* I have been grateful for the expert advice of a number of friends and colleagues, notably Mr Robin Hutchison the Keeper of the Scottish National Portrait Gallery: Mrs Helen Bennett and Mr Stuart Maxwell of the National Museum of Antiquities of Scotland; Mr R G Bonnington, Dr Margaret Sanderson, Miss Margaret Young, Mrs Pauline Maclean and their colleagues in the Scottish Record Office; Mr Iain Brown, Dr Paul Kelly and Mr John Morris of the National Library of Scotland; Miss Catherine H Cruft of the National Monuments Records and Mr David Sellar of the Department of Scots Law in the University of Edinburgh. Dr John Imrie, Keeper of the Records of Scotland, arranged for me to include in the exhibition privately owned documents deposited in the Scottish Record Office.

I would particularly thank all the owners who kindly lent to the exhibition pictures, documents and small objects from their collections, permitted the inclusion of these in this booklet and often provided most interesting additional information. Their names are noted in the list of exhibition lenders and their assistance has been much appreciated.

Finally, I would thank Mrs Sheila Smith for her excellent typing of this publication.

**Note on documentary sources.**

The abbreviation SRO in the references does not necessarily imply ownership by the Scottish Record Office but serves merely as an indication of the location of various documents, many of which are privately owned. The Right Honourable the Earl of Dalhousie, the Right Honourable the Earl of Leven and Melville, The Lord Polwarth, Sir John Clerk of Penicuik, Bt., Mrs J M Dick-Cunyngham and Messrs J and F Anderson WS, executors of the late Major P J K Blair Oliphant, and the Scottish Record Office have kindly given permission for extracts from their documents to be quoted here, as has His Grace the Duke of Hamilton, whose archives are at Lennoxlove.

# 1

# Education

A charming picture by David Allan shows the children of the Halkett of Pitfirrane family playing happily together, watched by their parents. Sons and daughters of the period certainly shared their leisure hours but they did not expect to receive the same education. After all, their future role in life was very different. A man had his living to make, be it in public affairs, in business or on the land. A girl's destiny was to marry and have children. Those domestic skills which she would need could best be acquired in her own family circle, from her mother. Education of an academic nature was totally irrelevant and in the earlier part of the seventeenth century at least there was no necessity for a woman to be able even to read and write.

In consequence, girls' education was much neglected. While the sons of noblemen, merchants, tradesmen and servants went to the local grammar school together, their sisters usually remained at home, helping to keep house and bring up the younger children. In certain parts of Scotland there were schools for girls, or schools which took both boys and girls, but such education was sporadic and ended early. If the sons of a noble family had a tutor the girls might share some lessons with them and there would always be those who took an intelligent interest in their brothers' books. To a large extent, however, the women of the first half of the seventeenth century were illiterate and even the daughters of the peerage

were obviously ill at ease when they had to set pen to paper: their spelling was frequently phonetic, their phraseology awkward.

By the 1670s the situation was changing. In imitation of the English pattern there was now an emphasis on the social accomplishments, on leisure pursuits suitable for a young lady. A girl from an aristocratic, professional or well-to-do business family was expected to be able to sing, play a musical instrument, dance, draw and do fine sewing. Something more than a mother's instruction was required and so boarding schools for girls became popular in Edinburgh. These were private establishments, teaching the desired skills along with some French, geography, arithmetic and a good deal of religious instruction. A few girls even studied Latin but they were in the minority for there was no attempt to produce the 'learned lady' so frowned upon by polite society.

**2** Lord Fountainhall's Account, 1670.
Extract from *Journals of Sir John Lauder, Lord Fountainhall*, ed. Donald Crawford (Scottish History Society 1900), 242.

*A dollar and a halfe given to a man for teaching my wife writing and arithmetick £14: 8/-.*

Leading lawyer though Lord Fountainhall might be, his wife had obviously come to him with little in the way of education and in this she was far from being unique. By the beginning of the eighteenth century, however, attitudes were changing as can be seen in this letter about Lady Anne Hamilton, motherless daughter of the Earl of

**1** Sir John Halkett of Pitfirrane Bart, and family, 1781, by David Allan.
Canvas: 60¼ × 94 inches (153 × 239 centimetres).
National Gallery of Scotland.

Ruglen. She was brought up by the Earl's house-keeper, Mrs Alcock, with the advice of his mother Anne, Duchess of Hamilton and his sister Susan, Marchioness of Tweeddale. The Duchess's companion, Mrs Montgomerie, frequently acted as intermediary.

*Hamilton February 14 1716*

*Madam . . .*

*I went Glasgow yesterday about sum little busines and sent the footman to Paislay to know how the yong ladys are and Mrs Alcock hearing I was at Glasgow she cam up and saw me to give a particolar accompt how the children are, which I was very glad of. Blised be God they are all very well. She is trowly a discreat servant and very concerned about them. She hes desired me to spek to My Lady Dutches [of Hamilton] and wryt to Your Ladyship that you wold have your thoughts about Lady Anne's education. Tho she is not so old, yet she is very big and womanly and it is pitty that nothing should be taught her that other ladys of her quality are teacht, such as wryting, dansing and Frainch, which she is very capable of and begins to be thoughfull about. It was leat this night befor I cam hom so that I have not got Her Grace spok to about this, but I shall do it and wryt to Your Ladyship what she says. It is lyk it does not ocur to her father at this time the capasity she hes for sum parts of education that should trowly be given her now. And if it be proper to sugest it to him, Your Ladyship will be best judge or if he be to com down [to Scotland] this sumer, you could better spek to him . . .*

3 Letter of Mrs Anna Montgomerie to Susan, Marchioness of Tweeddale, 1716.
National Library of Scotland, Yester Papers, MS 14419.

One young lady who did receive the desired education of the time was Janet Dick. Sir Alexander Dick and his wife lived with their young family at Prestonfield House, just outside Edinburgh. Their daughter Janet, born in 1749, was to be the sole survivor of their children and they brought her up with loving affection. When she was only five she had her portrait painted by the Edinburgh artist William Millar, who depicted her proudly holding up a favourite doll said to have been made for her by the elder Allan Ramsay. That Janet's education was entirely typical of her time is shown by a delightful and revealing letter which she wrote to her father in 1760. She was now eleven years old, her mother was in poor health and her lessons in household management therefore had more immediacy than would otherwise have been the case. Her letter is clearly written and, if the punctuation of the original is somewhat erratic, the spelling is good. So capable was Janet, indeed, that she had been put in charge of the household expenditure and each week the housekeeping money was paid to her. She was then expected to keep a careful record of exactly how it was spent.

On a lighter note, she could dance sufficiently well to be allowed to attend a public ball in Edinburgh, which she enjoyed in spite of a few moments of disquiet occasioned by having to manage the unfamiliar train of her dress. Her mother died later that same year but Janet's place as the cherished eldest daughter of the family remained secure after her father took a second wife and had several more children. By the time she was nineteen Janet numbered James Boswell the biographer among the admirers who came to Prestonfield on a Saturday evening to hear her sing and play. Vivacious and charming, she nonetheless refused the various suitors who proposed to her and remained unmarried, an accomplished and popular member of fashionable Edinburgh society.

**4** Janet Dick with her doll, 1754, by William Millar.
Canvas: 24 × 19 inches (60.9 × 48.2 centimetres)
Prestonfield House Hotel, Edinburgh.

[*Curiosities of a Scots Charta Chest 1600–1800*, ed. Mrs Atholl Forbes (Edinburgh 1897), 186.]

**5** Letter of Janet Dick to her father, Sir Alexander Dick, 1760.
SRO, Dick-Cunynghame of Prestonfield Muniments, GD 331/5/11.

*Prestonfield   March 8   1760*
*My Dear Papa,*
  *I wish I could tell you from my*
*heart what I'm sure you wish, which is Mamma's*
*good health which is at present very bad, but for partic-*
*ulars I refer you to Dr Rutherford who is to write*
*to you directly for your advice. We all thank you for*
*the new play. Whenever Mama is able to hear me I shall*
*read it to her. To be sure, it's fit I should, since My*
*Dear Parent recommended it to my perusal.*
  *Your health, which at present Mama is suspicious*
*of, makes us all ansious to hear about you. Sir, I*
*do ashure you your house book is in great order and not*
*one article escaped since you left us and I receive my anuity*
*every Saterday night, but I would rather have my*
*Dear Papa to see it and be satisfied with it than to*
*possess all the riches on earth. I am very proud when*
*when (sic) I can do anything to oblige you. My dear sister*
*Anne is the loveliest baby ever born. I must not*
*forget to tell you Mama let me go to Mr Lamole's ball. She*
*was not able to go with me but gave me in charge to Lady*
*McLeod, who took all good care of me. I was not the least*
*the worse of it. I danced with Lord Balgonie and they*
*say I danced very well. I was dressed in my green gown*
*with gold trimmings and nothing about me but what*
*you would have liked except my train, which was a little*
*troublesome, and if you don't like it when you come*
*home I shall sacrifice it. Cousin Peggy writes to you otherwise*
*mine should been longer. Dear Papa, I am your affectianote and*
    *obedient daughter,*
    *Janet Dick.*
*P.S. I am hurried with the post.*
  *Pardon my writing so horridly.*

Janet Dick was probably taught at home, but many of her contemporaries went to schools in Edinburgh of the kind run by Mrs Eupham Seton. This lady's name was actually incorporated into the design of a sampler worked by one of her young pupils, Betty Plenderleath, in 1745. The sampler was the most popular way of displaying a girl's skill with her needle, and Betty's typical designs of Adam and Eve, flowers and animals are worked on linen in cross, satin, Florentine, double-running, rococo, Algerian eye, rice and running stitches. Betty was perhaps the Elizabeth Plenderleith, daughter of an Edinburgh advocate, who married a Haddington merchant in 1758.

7 Cookery book: *A New and Easy Method of Cooking, by Elizabeth Cleland, chiefly intended for the benefit of the Young Ladies who attend her School* (Edinburgh 1755). SRO, Hume of Wedderburn Papers, GD 267/7/8.

**6** Betty Plenderleath's sampler, 1745.
$12\frac{1}{4} \times 9$ inches ($31.5 \times 23$ centimetres).
Royal Scottish Museum, 1939. $12\frac{1}{2}$.

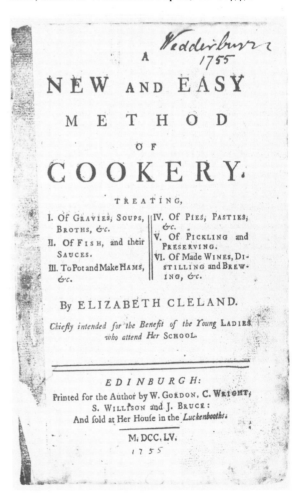

[See Margaret H Swain, *Historical Needlework* (London 1970), 78–9, Plate 48.]

Needlework pictures were almost as popular as samplers with young girls wishing to demonstrate their skill. The subject chosen was often biblical, as it is here. The offering of Isaac as a sacrifice by Abraham has been done in twisted silk, floss silk and purl on a woollen canvas background.

**8** Mary Man's needlework picture, early eighteenth century.
$12\frac{1}{2} \times 11\frac{1}{4}$ inches (31.7 × 28.6 centimetres).
National Museum of Antiquities of Scotland, MN 140.

Seated composedly at her spinet, apparently oblivious of her companion's intentions with a pair of scissors, is a young lady of about the year 1760. Although she is unidentified, her open book of music bears the heading 'Miss Nisbet's Reel' on the left hand page and so it seems likely that she is Mary Hamilton Nisbet (1750–1834) with her younger brother John. Whatever the identity of the children, the double portrait is a charming illustration of one facet of a girl's education.

Music had long been highly regarded as a feminine accomplishment, with the harpsichord, virginals, lute and guitar as favourite instruments. These were produced on the continent and in London, usually by French or German immigrants. There is as yet no firm evidence that musical instrument makers were at work in Scotland in the seventeenth century but contemporary accounts and customs records make it plain that all the popular instruments of the day were imported into this country.

**9** Two children at a spinet, *c.* 1760, by an unknown artist.
Canvas: $31\frac{3}{4} \times 52\frac{1}{4}$ inches (80.6 × 132.7 centimetres).
Sir David Ogilvy of Inverquharity, Bart.

The origin of the spinet in the portrait is recorded for all to see: clearly inscribed above the keyboard are the words 'Joseph Mahoon, London.' Mahoon was one of the first British-born makers of keyboard instruments. In his premises in Golden Square he manufactured both harpsichords and spinets. One of his harpsichords, indeed, features in a scene in Hogath's famous illustrations for 'The Rake's Progress'. The spinet shown here is of the English bent-side type popular at the end of the seventeenth century but still being produced by Mahoon in the 1740s and indeed later.

[G Thibault, Jean Jenkins and Josiane Bran-Ricci, *Eighteenth Century Musical Instruments: France and Britain* (Victoria and Albert Museum exhibition catalogue, London 1973), 6.]

Agnes Dalrymple, born on 11 September 1731, was the granddaughter of Sir David Dalrymple of Hailes. An heiress, she became the wife of Sir Gilbert Elliott of Minto when she was fifteen. She bore him seven children and they lived happily together for more than thirty years. She was only eight when Allan Ramsay painted her picture, yet she is clearly portrayed as an elegant young lady on the verge of adult life. Innocence and sophistication combine in this picture, which looks forward to her future as an eligible woman rather than back to the childhood she has scarcely left. In foreshadowing Agnes's own destiny, Ramsay's portrait at the same time epitomises the contemporary view of girlhood as a prelude to marriage.

**10** Agnes Murray-Kynynmond Dalrymple, 1739, by Allan Ramsay.
Canvas: $67\frac{1}{2} \times 39\frac{1}{4}$ inches ($171.5 \times 99.7$ centimetres).
In a Private Scottish Collection.

**11** Lord and Lady Jedburgh, *c.* 1685, by an unknown
artist: a marriage portrait.
Canvas: 43¼ × 49 inches (110.1 × 24.4 centimetres).
The Marquess of Lothian.

# 2

# Marriage

When a girl reached the age of sixteen or seventeen her parents began to give serious consideration to the problem of finding her a husband. In so doing, their main preoccupations were the property and status of the prospective bridegroom, especially if they themselves came from a wealthy or an aristocratic family. Their thoughts turned naturally to the young men of their own locality, even to cousins and other relatives. Normally, they took into account their daughter's wishes and in the seventeenth century there was a reasonable chance that their preferences and hers would coincide. Most girls enjoyed a very limited social life. Even those who left home to enter domestic service tended to do so in the households of friends and relations and therefore had few opportunities of meeting anyone outside their immediate family circle. They accordingly remained well within the sphere of parental influence, vulnerable to persuasion and pressure. It was towards the end of the century when girls were sent off to boarding school and allowed to attend public balls and functions in Edinburgh that they were more likely to meet young men unknown to their family and probably viewed by them with disapproval.

If matters proceeded according to plan, the parents would decide upon the suitable candidate and enter into discussions with his family. Once an agreement was reached, a marriage contract was drawn up. Such documents were not merely the prerogative of the very rich who had a great deal of property to consider. On the contrary, the marriage contracts of farmers, merchants, lawyers, shopkeepers, tradesmen and servants still survive. The contract, after all, was what provided much of a wife's future legal and financial security.

The actual document followed a set form and although it was a long one, often consisting of several pages joined together vertically to form a scroll, its basic provisions were few. First came the young couple's promise to marry before a certain date—which was often left blank. The bride's father would then provide her with a tocher (dowry). This would be paid to her husband in two or three instalments after the marriage had taken place and there was often a penalty clause for delay. In return, the groom's father usually settled upon the bride and groom the jointure, a piece of land or property giving an annual revenue. If her husband died before her, the jointure was her means of subsistence.

Linked to the tocher of the bride were the provisions made for any daughters she might have. For example, if her own tocher was £10,000 Scots, an only daughter of her marriage would receive the same sum. If she had two daughters, the elder would have £6,000, the younger £4,000. If there were three girls, they would be given, say, £4,500, £3,500 and £2,000 respectively. These sums of money were payable when the girls reached a stated age—usually sixteen or eighteen—or when they married. Some contracts had additional clauses specifying minor points but for the most part the basic arrangements for tocher, jointure and daughters' provisions were what mattered.

The signing of the contract was often a ceremony in itself, held in the presence of family and friends. The marriage followed soon afterwards. It was often solemnised at the bride's home and was accompanied by much rejoicing, the music and feasting continuing for more than a week. Finally, the young couple departed to begin their married life together, frequently in the household of the bridegroom's father.

The family arrangements forming the background to an engagement are reflected in a letter Isabel Gray wrote to her dead sister's husband, John Clerk, about a suitor for her niece. Although the young man was unknown to Clerk, he was a relative of Isabel Gray's husband and she had obviously inquired carefully into his background before agreeing to make an approach to the Clerk family.

**12** Letter of Isabel Gray to John Clerk of Penicuik, 1670.
SRO, Clerk of Penicuik Papers, GD 18/5171/10.

*Loving Brother,*
*   There is a gentelman that hes seen your daughter Mary Clerk that they*
*call Robert Campbell, son to Collen Campbell in Glasgow. Hee is written to*
*John Campbel and is very desireous to come to Edinburgh or Pennicook to*
*see her if you would admite of it. Hee is a very sober, discrete yong man and*
*his father will give him a considerable portion and he is a very good merchand*
*and hes been abroad and is said to be very very vertous gentelman. You may*
*send in Mary to Edinburgh if you pleas, which is more conveinent to see her here.*
*I desire your answere with this bearer. Mistres Yong will tell her mind about*
*that gentelman. I remember my service to your wif. I am*
*                          Your affectionat*
*Edinburgh                 sister and servant,*
*10 March 1670             Issobell Gray*

The strong, practical considerations underlying so many marriages were particularly evident when a widower sought a wife. Because so many women died in childbirth, men were frequently left with with young families to bring up. Sometimes an unmarried sister could come to the rescue, sometimes the children were left to the care of the servants, but most men took the obvious course of action and remarried.

One of those who did was Robert Dundas, then Lord Advocate of Scotland and later Lord President of the Court of Session. At the age of twenty-eight he had married an heiress who brought him not only her fortune but great domestic happiness. Fourteen years later she died, leaving him with four small daughters. Although heartbroken to lose her, he began almost at once to look for a second wife among his immediate circle of legal friends. He soon settled upon Jean Grant, the third daughter of Lord Prestongrange, his predecessor as Lord Advocate.

The motives for this marriage are made clear in a letter written to him by his friend Lord Hopetoun. 'Dear Robin', the latter began, 'I have talked over your affair fully with my friend and well-wisher. We both agree in applauding the measure in general, not only as rational but even necessary in your situation and I think it will be extremely lucky for your young family, especially the eldest, if they fall soon into such hands as we would wish for a meet help to you. A woman of prudence, good nature, temper, activity, economy etc etc. And for the sake of the dear baby we would have her heart remarkably good, generous and disinterested. Nothing less will please. But how the person in view may come up to this character is what we are absolutely ignorant of, which we regret, because had we any access to know it, nothing should be concealed from you in a point of such consequence, and where it is so difficult for you to come at the truth, even tho' your acquaintance had been longer and more intimate than it has been, or tho' she herself had been better known to the world. So that we can only add our best wishes that everything may be directed for the best.'

Dundas did not take long to make up his mind, for he married Jean in September 1756. Her portrait, painted in the following year, shows a homely looking girl with a kind expression. She settled down happily with her husband and his daughters, and herself bore him four sons and two more daughters.

[*The Arniston Memoirs* ed. George W T Omond (Edinburgh 1887), 160 *et seq*.]

**13** Jean Grant, Lady Dundas, 1757, by Andrea Soldi. Canvas: 50 × 40 inches (127 × 101.6 centimetres). In a Private Scottish Collection.

Although so many Scotsmen married local girls it should not be forgotten that there were those who found their wives elsewhere. A number of English, Irish, Dutch and French girls married into Scottish families and a proportion of them actually came and settled in their husband's country rather than the husband making his home in their part of the world. One such was Lady Mary Moore, second daughter of the Earl of Drogheda.

Portrayed by Lely as a confident young beauty, Lady Mary married William, 3rd Earl of Dalhousie and became the mother of three sons and a daughter. By marrying into the Scottish peerage she became part of it, one of those ladies who in their own private sphere introduced the customs and aspirations of a rather different society. When her husband died after only a few years she again married a Scotsman, becoming the wife of John, 2nd Lord Bellenden. In addition to the five sons she bore him, she had two more daughters, both of whom were to be celebrated Court beauties in their day. Widowed for a second time, she married a medical doctor named Samuel Collins.

**14** Mary, Countess of Dalhousie, *c.* 1675, by Sir Peter Lely. Canvas: 50 × 40 inches (127 × 101.6 centimetres). Colin Broun Lindsay Esq of Colstoun.

*Accompt His Grace the Duke of Hamiltone for Cloathes furnished to My Ladie Margarat at her wedding, be James Row   4th February 1687.*

| | £ | s | d |
|---|---|---|---|
| *Imprimis, 22 ells ritch whit saten at £9 ell for goun and piticot and lyneing* | 198 | | |
| *½ ell ditto for sho maker* | 4 | 10 | |
| *8 ells crimson ditto for nightgoune [dressing gown]* | 52 | 16 | |
| *8 ells whit ditto for lyneing it £5 : 8/- ell* | 43 | 4 | |
| *⅜ ells ditto* | 2 | | 6 |
| *1⅛ ells ditto for stayes at £5 : 8/- ell* | 6 | 1 | 6 |
| *18¾ ells blak velvet for goun £12 ell* | 225 | | |
| *6¾ ells crimson velvet for piticot £13 : 4/-* | 89 | 2 | |
| *5 ells crimsone ribin for the tale [tail]* | 1 | 10 | |
| *2 ells whit tafaty for pockets and lyneing goun bodies etc at £4  10/-* | 9 | | |
| *1 rune hood at* | 4 | | |
| *1 twilted [quilted] basket at* | 10 | | |
| *1 twilted piticoat [quilted petticoat] and westcoat* | 30 | | |
| *1 pair laced shooes at* | 2 | 16 | |
| *1 pair whit glazed kids [gloves] at* | 1 | 10 | |
| *6 boxwood combes at 16/-* | 4 | 16 | |
| *5 paper[s] preens [pins] at 6/6 paper* | 1 | 12 | 6 |
| *1 Romanie parle [pearl] necklace* | 1 | 4 | |
| | 1714 | 16 | 6 |

Preparations for a large wedding naturally went on for many weeks before the actual ceremony. The bride herself was much taken up with the gathering together of garments and furnishings to take to her new home. The clothing purchased by Lady Margaret Hamilton, the 3rd Duke of Hamilton's youngest daughter, for her marriage to James, Earl of Panmure is recorded in an Edinburgh tailor's account. The rich white satin gown was no doubt the actual wedding dress.

[See Rosalind K Marshall, 'Three Scottish Brides 1670–87' in *Costume* (1974), viii, 43–5.]

**15** Extract from the account for the trousseau of Lady Margaret Hamilton, Countess of Panmure, 1687. Hamilton Archives F2/492/3.

**16** A Highland Wedding, *c.* 1782, engraved after a
painting by David Allan.
In a Private Scottish Collection.

No picture of a seventeenth or early eighteenth
century Scottish marriage ceremony has come to
light, but an engraving after a picture by David
Allan shows something of the attendant festivities.
His scene is set in the Highlands and the bride
wears a plaid while the men are in Highland dress.
Although Lowland weddings were different in
detail the sense of rejoicing was no doubt the same.
Here, the bride's companions break bread over
her head in a gesture symbolising good fortune.
Musicians play in the background, men fire off
guns in salute and toasts are already being drunk.

**17** Column commemorating the marriage of Lady
Margaret Hamilton to James, Earl of Panmure.
Erected by the Earl, 1699.
Photograph by the Royal Commission on Ancient
Monuments, Scotland, AN/472.

**18** Lintel stone above a doorway in Dysart, Fife. Photograph by the Royal Commission on Ancient Monuments, Scotland, MW/BR/DYS(T)/62.

Rare indeed was a marriage commemorated by an imposing monument, but it was quite customary in certain areas of Scotland for the initials of husband and wife to be recorded on a more modest scale on furniture and also above doorways in the form of carved lintels. Particularly in the eastern burghs of Fife the commemorative lintel stone was common, usually ornamented with the date of the building and a heart as well as the initials.

**19** David Smythe and his wife, 1761, by F Lindo. Canvas: $33\frac{1}{2} \times 43$ inches ($85.1 \times 90.2$ centimetres). In a Private Scottish Collection.

Another pleasing way of marking a marriage was to commission a portrait of bride and groom. Although few Scottish double portraits of this kind are extant, enough remain to suggest that the custom found as much favour here as it did in the south throughout the period under consideration. The picture of Lord and Lady Jedburgh is presumably a marriage portrait and so too is the picture of Mr and Mrs Smythe of Methven. David Smythe was fifty when he married for a second time in 1761. His bride was Catherine Campbell, the daughter of Patrick Campbell, one of the Senators of the College of Justice. In the year of their wedding their portrait was painted. Both are arrayed in their best garments, he in his smart suit, she in her elegant yellow, sack-back dress. Their clothes are more suited to an evening entertainment in Edinburgh but the artist has conceived the attractive idea of placing them in the grounds of Methven Castle, with Mr Smythe half turning to indicate to his bride her new home.

**20** Janet Dick, 1748, by Allan Ramsay.
Canvas: 30 × 25 inches (76.2 × 63.5 centimetres).
Prestonfield House Hotel, Edinburgh.

Not all marriage arrangements proceeded according to a settled plan, of course, and it is interesting to note how many times sons and daughters asserted their will. Strong-minded girls were often determined to have their own way, with the result that there were tearful scenes, mutual recriminations, elopements and clandestine mar-

riages. One couple who stood out against family opposition were Janet Dick and Sandy Cunynghame, parents of the small girl whose education is discussed in Section 1.

Sandy studied medicine at Edinburgh and Leyden, then eventually returned from the continent to practise in Pembrokeshire. When he was thirty-three he came back to Scotland, met his cousin's daughter Janet Dick and they fell in love, only to encounter their parents' obstinate determination that they should not marry. Possibly the age difference was the cause of the trouble: marriage with a near relative was quite usual in Scotland. At any rate, persuasion and pleadings were in vain. The old people's 'hearts were hard as the rocks', Sandy commented later, but he and Janet were not to be so easily deterred. Abandoning the subject of marriage, he told his father that he had a notion to travel to Italy with his old friend Allan Ramsay the portrait painter. His father seized upon what he saw as a welcome diversion and encouraged him to go. A trip to Paris and Rome would soon put all thoughts of Janet out of his son's head. In the event, the young couple married secretly on the eve of Sandy's departure, telling only Allan Ramsay's father and one other friend of the wedding.

Janet remained at home in Clermiston with her parents, consoled by letters from the continent conveyed to her by the Ramsay family. Eventually the news of the marriage leaked out and the Cunynghames refused to have anything to do with their son. As time passed, however, their attitude softened and on Sandy's return after a year's absence there was the desired reconciliation.

In 1746 Sandy inherited a baronetcy, adopted the name Sir Alexander Dick and moved his family to Prestonfield House. His new home became a favourite visiting place for a wide circle of literary, artistic and scientific friends. Allan Ramsay the artist was a frequent visitor and it was he who painted Janet's portrait in 1748, the year before her daughter Janet was born. Sadly, the household at Prestonfield in the 1750s was overshadowed by Lady Dick's ill-health. She did not recover from the birth of her youngest child and on 26 December 1760 she died at Prestonfield, leaving family and friends bereft of 'a most bewitching companion.'

[Mrs Atholl Forbes, *Curiosities of a Scots Charta Chest* 1600–1800 (Edinburgh 1897), *passim*.]

**21** Letter of Sandy Cunynghame (later Sir Alexander Dick) to his wife Janet Dick ('Jessy'), 1737. SRO, Dick-Cunynghame of Prestonfield Muniments, GD 331/40/2.

**22** Margaret Lindsay, Mrs Allan Ramsay, 1754–5, by Allan Ramsay.
Canvas: 30 × 25 inches (76.2 × 63.5 centimetres).
National Gallery of Scotland.

*Milan April 6 N.S.*
*1737*

*My dearest Jessy, Love, Wife and everything*
*else that is dear to me,*
　　*You may expect that by the*
*time you read this I am more than half way home,*
*being just now on my journey and at least four*
*hundred miles nearer you than when I was at Rome.*
*I came over the Alps to the tune of 'The Last Time*
*I came o'er the Moor I left my Love behind me'.*
*I leave you to sing the rest of it. No more over*
*the hills and far away, but down the burn, Jessy Love*
*and I will follow thee. I vow to God I have*
*not been merry since I left you till I set my face*
*homewards in hopes of seeing you. I have often wisht*
*for the wings of a dove to flye like lightning and perch*
*upon your throne among the Braes of Clermy where I*
*might accidentally met you with your book in your hand*
*and pick round about the ground where you walkt.*
*Dear Life, I wrote a letter to My Father and drew a bill*
*upon him when I left Rome. God knows what the effect*
*will be or if he will pay my bill. I was streightened*
*on all sides to get money to come home else I would not have*
*troubled him. I cannot yet get a farthing of Mr Livingston's*
*money till the courts meet at London but when I come there*
*(God willing) I will make it my first bussiness to pay all my*
*debt tho you and I shoud have but a shilling a day to live*
*upon.*
*It is not the first time we have done so . . .*
*In the meantime, do all you can as it lyes in your way to*
*show all due respect and complaisance to our Mother and*
*Father.*
*Your prudent and wise behaviour is all I now have to*
*promote a reconciliation. I have not the least doubt but that*
*every day you consider how you may do and say obligding*
*things to them, for this is wisdom, prudence and everything*
*that can lend to make us happy. My Dearest Life, keep*
*hearty and well, for I shall never rest till I be at home*
*and be yours for ever.*
　　　　　*Sandy Cunynghame.*

Several years after his friend Sandy Cunynghame's clandestine marriage, Allan Ramsay the portrait painter was himself at the centre of a romantic episode. His first wife had died at their London home in 1743 giving birth to a daughter and all his children of that marriage were to die young. It took him a long time to recover from these personal tragedies, but in 1751 while he was visiting Scotland he met a young woman named Margaret Lindsay. The eldest daughter of Sir Alexander Lindsay of Evelick in Perthshire, Margaret was not only sweet-natured and sympathetic but she possessed sound business abilities. The tradition that the Lindsays employed Ramsay as their daughter's drawing master seems to be fanciful, but there is no doubt that they disapproved of him as a suitor. A portrait painter, however successful, was scarcely an appropriate match for the daughter of an old landed family. They would not hear of an engagement so Ramsay and Margaret eloped to Edinburgh where they were married in the Canongate Church on 1 March 1752.

In spite of persuasive letters from the young couple and their friends, Margaret's parents refused to forgive them. 'That I have cause to be displeased with my daughter is undeniable, as she has done the most undutiful act was in her power to do', Sir Alexander declared, adding, 'I therefore think I am bound to do the duty of a parent in letting her see that an affair of that consequence, if done without consent (even though otherwise respectable) is not to be too easily forgiven.' It was not until after his death many years later that Margaret was able to see her mother again.

Meanwhile, she had gone south with her husband to settle in London. Eight months later she gave birth to premature twins, who survived for only a few hours, but in the following years she presented her husband with a son and two daughters. Her practical good sense was a great asset to him in his business affairs and it was she who managed his finances. She accompanied him on his travels abroad and it was while they were in Italy in 1754–5 that he painted the serene portrait of her shown here. She lived until 1782, her husband surviving her by two years.

[Alastair Smart, *The Life and Art of Allan Ramsay* (London 1952), *passim*.]

**23** Letter of Sophia Clerk to her father Sir John Clerk of Penicuik, 1702.
SRO, Clerk of Penicuik Papers, GD 18/5250/2.

*Dir Father,*
   *Since my presant sirecumstancess hes oblidged me*
*to be in the countrie for a fewe dayes I could*
*no go hom without giveing you this*
*small tocken of my respectt. I knowe very well*
*that may [ie my] letter shall be rather grievousse to you*
*then acceptable since it will putt you in mind [of]*
*so unhappy a cretuer as I am. I know very well*
*how greati reason you have to be offended at me*
*but God pitty me it is what I cannot help nowe*
*wherfor I must suffer patiently since I meyself*
*have been the only cause of may misfortiones.*
*I can never expect you will be reconsiled to*
*me only I beg that at eny time you reflect on my*
*neglect of deuty to you that you wold forgive*
*me. Pardon the troublee this leter mey give*
*to you for tho you shall never lock upon*
*me yet I will be upon my douty and alwayes*
*wish you well whiell I breath*
                    *Your[r] affectianat*
*End.                    doghter til death*
*October 10 day 1702        Sophi Clerk*

In the spring of 1702 Sophia Clerk eloped with a young merchant named Gabriel Little. Her father had done everything in his power to stop her from marrying one whom he described as 'a beggar and a madman', even urging a friend to tie her up and feed her with bread and water in an attempt to restrain her. Sophia was headstrong, though, and she went through with the marriage. Some months later she wrote Sir John a contrite letter, hoping for a reconciliation. He did forgive her, but her marriage was not the success she expected. (See Section 3)

**24** The Douglas Chair, 1665.
National Museum of Antiquities of Scotland, KN9.

Oak armchair made for Sir William Douglas, 2nd Baronet of Glenbervie and his wife Anne Douglas, with the Douglas genealogical tree carved on the back panel and the initials of husband and wife.

# 3

# Husbands and Wives

When a young woman married, her legal position altered radically. As one modern authority has put it, 'On marriage the husband acquired power over the person of his wife, who was considered to have no legal *persona*. As ruler of the house, he had control of her person and conduct, including the assigning of a place of residence.' In most cases, the wife's moveable property passed under her husband's complete control and even if she did have an estate of her own, his consent was necessary before she could take any action affecting it. She was also unable to enter into personal obligations and her husband even became liable for the debts she had contracted before her marriage. These changes in her position explain why the marriage contract was such an important document. It safeguarded her financial future and in many cases modified the husband's legal rights over her personal property.

Wedded to a man of her family's choosing, with many of her legal rights transferred to him, what prospect of happiness could a woman have as a wife? The answer is a surprisingly optimistic one. Apart from the fact that the element of choice she enjoyed has often been underestimated, a girl who had grown up expecting an arranged marriage did not normally cherish many romantic illusions about matrimony. She accepted the situation and was prepared to do her best to make the union a

successful one. Indeed, contemporary documents make it clear that in many instances a tender mutual affection grew up between husband and wife.

Nor was the wife a completely submissive partner in the relationship. Of course, there were dominating husbands who wished to supervise every aspect of their wives' existence, but there were also forceful women who ruled their families with a firm hand. Much depended upon personality and for the most part the arranged marriage was a successful partnership, albeit an unequal one in the face of the law.

When things did go wrong, little could be done to remedy the situation. The only two grounds for divorce were adultery and desertion. Adultery had since the Reformation been regarded as a heinous crime and in its most flagrant forms in the sixteenth century had even been punishable by death. The innocent party was entitled to all rights as though the other partner were dead, but regardless of who had been the offender the tocher remained in the husband's possession. Divorce for desertion was a lengthy business involving a whole series of actions in different courts. Unless a woman had powerful relatives to support her, she was unlikely to be in a position to initiate divorce proceedings. More usual were legal separations. Cruelty did not form grounds for divorce since it was regarded as being an abuse of the normal difficulties encountered in marriage but in extreme cases the courts would intervene to protect the life or health of the injured party. A maltreated wife could therefore apply for a decree of separation which allowed her to live apart from her husband although the marriage bond remained undissolved.

**25** Sir Archibald Grant and his 1st wife, Anne Hamilton, 1727, by John Smibert.
Canvas: 56 × 66 inches (142.2 × 167.7 centimetres).
The Testamentary Trustees of the late Sir F C Grant, Bt.

**26** Lord and Lady Belhaven, *c.* 1643, from the studio of Sir Anthony Van Dyck.
Canvas: 49 × 57¾ inches (124.5 × 146.7 centimetres).
Scottish National Portrait Gallery

One husband who owed much to his wife's ingenuity was Lord Belhaven. Born Margaret Hamilton, Lady Belhaven was the half-sister of the 1st Duke of Hamilton. Although she was illegitimate, her parentage was recognised and her ties with her father's family were strengthened still further when she married Sir John Hamilton of Broomhill, later Lord Belhaven and himself a descendant of the 1st Lord Hamilton.

It was not surprising, therefore, to find that during the Civil War Lord Belhaven was, along with Hamilton, an active supporter of the Royalist cause. Indeed, in 1647 he accompanied the Duke's expedition into England in an attempt to rescue Charles I. The army was defeated and both Hamilton and the King were eventually executed. Lord Belhaven escaped, but his troubles were not at an end. He had acted as surety for large debts contracted by the Duke, and in the early 1650s it seemed that his creditors would seize his own

lands, probably having him imprisoned for debt.

It was at this point that Lady Belhaven came to the rescue. Described by a contemporary as 'a very cuthie woman' she was sensible, energetic and much relied upon by the rest of the family for medical advice in particular, her skill with herbs being well known. It would also seem that she was of an inventive turn of mind. She and her husband discussed his difficulties. She outlined a plan and he agreed. Shortly afterwards he set out for England, accompanied by one servant. Making sure that everyone knew of his journey, he declared he would take the western route which involved crossing the treacherous estuary of the River Solway, notorious for its fickle tides.

He was last seen riding towards the river. Some time later, his distraught servant returned leading his master's horse and carrying his sodden hat. Lord Belhaven, he announced sadly, had been carried away while trying to cross the river. Lady Belhaven and her friends made a great display of grief. Everyone accepted that her husband was dead. All the legal documents of the time refer to him as the deceased Lord Belhaven and, of course, his creditors were foiled: Lady Belhaven was

entitled to retain his estates for herself and her children.

Nearly seven years passed. Occasionally there were odd rumours to the effect that Lady Belhaven was entertaining a secret visitor, but this was passed off as idle gossip. She remained quietly at home with her son, seeing her married daughters frequently. Then came the Restoration and to the amazement of everyone Lord Belhaven reappeared. Resuming his position as head of his family, he explained that, following his wife's advice, he had arranged his own apparent demise. He had, in fact, crossed the Solway safely and had made his way south, revealing his identity to no one. He had found employment as a gardener, keeping his true identity secret and paying only the occasional visit home—hence his wife's mysterious caller.

**27** Letter of Katherine Hume to her husband the laird of Kimmerghame, 1669.
SRO, Hume of Marchmont Papers, GD 158/2720/17.

Many of the women's letters which are extant were written by wives to absent husbands, combining personal solicitousness with a discussion of domestic requirements.

*My dearest,*
*  I am in such counfusion at your staying*
*so long from me that I know not what*
*to wret bot to obey you and to let you he[a]r*
*we are al wel, only I want my dear's plea-*
*sant conversation which is beter to me nor*
*health ore any other thing in this world.*
*Tibi is preti wel. She hath had a gret flux*
*which I think hath done*
*her much good. She is wel plesed with her*
*bodies [ie bodices] and I as ele [ie ill]. I have sent mine*
*back again for they are so stret [ie tight] that I*
*cannot wear them, besed [ie besides] they are soe*
*slight that I beleve they wad not lest [ie last]*
*two munths, therfor I intret you gar [ie cause]*
*give them back agin and get me a*
*per of strong twel [ie twill] ones if there be*
*ony. If not, let them alone and I shal*
*get them at Kelso. I rest in hast*
*                me ever dearest,*
*                your obedient wife*
*                Kathrine Hume*
*15 November 1669*

**28** Letter of David, 3rd Earl of Leven to his wife Lady Anna Wemyss, 1692.
SRO, Leven and Melville Papers, GD 26/13/420.

More than a hundred of the letters of David Earl of Leven to his wife Lady Anna Wemyss survive to demonstrate the strength of their affection for each other. They had married in 1691 when the Earl was thirty-one and his bride rather younger. Possibly his active military career had not left him with the opportunity of taking a wife before then. Their first child, Mary, was born the following July. While the Countess recovered from the birth, the Earl went on a hunting trip to Dumfriesshire, sending home affectionate notes like the one which follows.

*Muffat  July 23*
*My Dearest Heart,*
*  I am very glad you are growing strong.*
*It's fitt you be so befor the young*
*laird be gotten, so pray be carefull*
*of yourselfe. In time, My Dearest,*
*I shall make all the haist home I*
*can but you know ther's never less*
*need for the husband's being at home*
*then when the wife is in your*
*condition. My Dearest Heart, you*
*are dearer to me now since you*
*have suffered so much for me and*
*my child then ever you was and*
*it's indeed but just that so good a*
*wife as you are should have as*
*loving and affectionat a husband*
*as is, my Dearest Heart, yours.*

**29** Letter of Anna, Countess of Leven to her husband the Earl, *c.* 1694.
SRO, Leven and Melville Papers, GD 26/13/418.

**30** Letter of John, 16th Earl of Mar to his first wife Lady Margaret Hay, 1705.
SRO, Mar and Kellie Muniments, GD 124/15/231/14.

*My Dearest Heart*
   *I have sent you two letters that the*
*north country post brought here*
*lait this afternoon, but ther came*
*none from Moniemeall els I had sent*
*them after you, as desired. My*
*Dearest Heart, if you be not to come*
*over tomorrow, send me word, that I may*
*have the satisfaction to hear from*
*you if I cannot see you. I have*
*been pritty well all this day, some-*
*times troubled with pains but that's nothing.*
*I beg you, have a cair of yourself, my*
*sweet thing. I'm sure you will if*
*you regard the quite [ie quiet] or life of your*
*poor daft wife. It's very lait, so*
          *Adieu my dearest,*
*Fryday night*

*My Dear Magie*
   *I went yesterday morning and got your*
*china in Crokets and choised your 2 dussan glasses in*

*went to Jense and gave her your letter and beg'd her to go and*
*see for the rest of the things you wrote for, except the*
*meat. I sent Nodding and Roger to wait of her. All is*
*sent by the bearer as you'll see by Jense letter and four*
*water carafs beside which I caused get today. She has sent*
*you the bills. Send them back to me and I'll pay them. I*
*thought it best to send you out thir things tho the*
*company were not to be with you because you wou'd want*
*them. However and perhaps you'll get your viset Saturday*
*nixt, tho not if I can shun it han'somely. I was full*
*of the thoughts of seeing you today, but to my griff*
*the Parliament sits today and I believe will do so on*
                    *Munday too,*
*so it was imposible to do it. However, ther's one comfort,*
*that our sitting so frequently now will make the*
*Parliament sooner at an end. My dear life, be not vext at my*
*not comeing, for you see I cou'd not help it, but assure your-*
*self that as soon as I can have so much time for the*
*Parliament I will be with you, for I long as much for it*
                    *as you do.*

                *My dearest life, I am*
                      *Yours*
*Edinburgh Saturday 11 aclock*
   *August 23rd 1705*
*I'm sorie I was not the bearer of this myself and*
*I know you'll be disapointed when you get it in place*
*of me, but, Dear Magie, I cou'd not help it and it*
*troubles me as much as it will do you.*

Involved as he was in public affairs, the Earl of Mar nonetheless found time to see to various domestic purchases required by his eighteen year old wife.

Another affectionate and successful marriage was that of Janet Inglis and Sir John Clerk of Penicuik. Sir John had originally married a daughter of the Earl of Galloway and her death in childbirth ten months later left him heartbroken. For eight years he remained a widower until, 'by some secret charm or order of divine providence I settled my thoughts on Mistress Janet Inglis of Cramond'. Janet was the third daughter of Sir James Inglis and her husband later recorded that 'she had been educated under a most verteous mother, daughter of Sir Patrick Houston, and was herself what I always hope to find her, a most religious, verteous woman and one who in all respects might suit my humure and circumstances to rub through the world in a sober and privat[e] state of life.' He gained his father's approval then, 'after haveing gone through a few formalities of courtship', he was married on 15 February 1709. His wife was about twenty-two, he ten years older.

They suited each other admirably and Janet's loving letters to him after twenty years of married life survive to this day. They spent a few weeks in hired lodgings in Edinburgh, moved in with Sir John's father at Penicuik for some months then finally acquired their own house in Edinburgh. Their first son, born on 2 December 1709, was followed by fifteen other children. Janet's diary for these years consists mainly of religious reflections interspersed with comments on the health of her family. After the death of Sir John's father they moved to Penicuik then built a new home for themselves at Mavisbank. Their life together was unexceptional, punctuated by no romantic episodes, but by any standards their marriage was a happy and successful one which was to endure for over forty-five years until Sir John's death in 1755.

**31** Janet Inglis, Lady Clerk, *c.* 1712, by William Aikman.
Canvas: 30 × 25 inches (76.2 × 63.5 centimetres).
Sir John Clerk of Penicuik, Bt.

**32** Letter of Janet Inglis to her husband Sir John Clerk, 1718.
SRO, Clerk of Penicuik Papers, GD 18/5289/7.

*Pennycook*
*Jully 25*

*My Dearest,*
*I shall always receive any*
*present you shall pleas to*
*give me with pleasure and*
*thankfullness. You will remember*
*to look for chairs to the purple*
*room. I've wrot[e] to Mrs Shaw to*
*send out her man and camblet*
*to hang the room. I'm affraid*
*our covering below the table which*
*hath served us this great while*
*is not fitt for Dukes and Dutches*
*so and you pleas my Lady Inglis is*
*the fittest hand to buy on[e] of the*
*painted cloaths and one for*
*the side board. I shall mind*
*the wine aganst Saterday.*
*Adiew my Dear*
*Archie Lawther is engag'd*
*to go to Auchindinie's service*
*this week. I shall have your coat reddy.*

ation of George III but the Earl was delicate and a retired life suited him best so he soon returned to Scotland with his Countess.

In 1764 the couple's first child, a daughter, was born, to be followed by another in 1765. The elder child died early the next year and the Countess was by now increasingly worried about her husband's health. She persuaded him to pay a visit to Bath to take the waters but in May 1766 she had to send word home that he was seriously ill. 'I hope you will not be surprised at my not writing to you', she told her correspondent 'when I tell you that these sixteen nights past I have not had my cloaths off and have never been able to leave his bedside. He

**33** Letter of Christian Kilpatrick to her sixty-eight year old husband Sir John Clerk of Penicuik, 1718. SRO, Clerk of Penicuik Papers, GD 18/5254/11/1.

Janet Inglis's mother-in-law had been equally concerned for her husband's welfare.

*My dearest,*
*I received yours this afternoon*
*and am sorie your business will not alow you to come*
*home this week. As for my coming in, it is neidles*
*seeing the Baron and his lady are to be in town the*
*nixt week to stay, so I cannott be so ussfull to*
*you as you were allowing, and have no busines that*
*I will come in for of my own. I hope they will take*
*a care of you while they are there, for I hear how*
*you live and neglects yourself daylie by boylling*
*your hens which make very sober broth.*

*I send you in a wild goos and two good hens. I pray*
*do not give away the goos but make it ready for your*
*self and get some comerad to bear you company. It is*
*a little on[e] but prety good of that kind . . .*

*Your affectionat and*
*obediant wife*
*Christian Kilpatrick*

*Newbiging*
*24 January 1718*

**34** Lady Mary Maxwell, Countess of Sutherland, c. 1761, by Allan Ramsay.
Canvas: 30 × 25 inches (76.2 × 63.5 centimetres).
The Countess of Sutherland

In an age of high mortality death cut short all too many marriages. Often it was the wife who died prematurely, usually in childbirth, but it was the 17th Earl of Sutherland's early death which terminated his happy marriage. In April 1761 he had married Mary Maxwell, eldest daughter and co-heiress of William Maxwell of Preston. Five months later they were in London for the coron-

has had a dreadful fever and I'm afraid his delicate constitution will not stand [it], tho' the worst symptoms begin to leave him.'

Sad to say, her devoted nursing had tragic consequences for herself. She caught the fever and on 1 June she died. The Earl lingered on for another fortnight but on 16 June he too died. They were buried together at Holyrood in the same grave, their year-old daughter inheriting the family titles and estates.

[W Fraser, *Memorials of the Family of Wemyss of Wemyss* (Edinburgh 1888) iii, 222.]

**35** Christian Shairp, 1750, by Allan Ramsay.
Canvas: 30 × 25 inches (76.2 × 63.5 centimetres).
Mrs Tam Dalyell of the Binns.

The marital problems confronting Christian Shairp were posed by ill-health of a rather different kind. Christian was the elder daughter of Thomas Shairp of Houston. For many years she remained unmarried, occupying the role of the typical spinster daughter who stayed at home and helped run the household. One of her father's servants bore witness to her kindly nature at this period when, in appreciation of her concern for him, he left her all his possessions.

The circumstances of Christian's late marriage remain obscure, but when she was well into her forties she became the wife of a retired naval captain, Peter Forbes. He had nothing more than his half pay to live on, but there was Christian's dowry of 20,000 merks to help out. At first they stayed in Scotland but about 1777 they moved south to settle near London. By now Captain Forbes was showing signs of mental derangement and Christian was finally forced to conclude that she could no longer look after him herself. As her lawyers later put it, he was placed 'in a private receptacle for lunatics' near London and there he remained for the rest of his life. Realising that there was no hope of his recovery, Christian decided to return to her friends in Scotland. She bought herself a small house in the New Town of Edinburgh and she lived there until her death on 7 December 1799. Captain Forbes survived her by only nineteen days.

[SRO, Shairp of Houston Muniments, GD 30/2049/3, GD 30/889.]

**36** Rachel Chiesly, Lady Grange, c. 1705, by Sir John Medina.
Canvas: $30\frac{1}{4} \times 24\frac{5}{8}$ inches ($76.8 \times 62.4$ centimetres).
The Earl of Mar and Kellie: on loan to the Scottish National Portrait Gallery.

The story of Rachel, Lady Grange illustrates vividly the difficulties which arose when the relationship between a husband and wife broke down. Lord Grange, younger brother of the Earl of Mar, was a lawyer of an introspective, self-doubting temperament. By his own account, he fell deeply in love with Rachel Chiesly. His choice could hardly have been more unsuitable, for Rachel's father had been the man who assassinated the Lord President of the Court of Session, Sir George Lockhart, after the latter had given judgment against him in a lawsuit. Lord Grange's friends were quick to point out that the marriage would ruin his prospects and he himself later admitted, 'I believe I would have left her notwithstanding I lov'd her so much, had it not been that I thought it dirty and villainous and that I could not perfidiously break the many oaths I had given her that I would never forsake her.'

They were married in secret and when Lady Grange later alleged that they 'lived near twenty-five years in great love and peace' it seems that she was stating no more than the truth. Her husband's journal for 1718 is still in existence and reflects a perfectly normal married life. Beneath the apparent calm, however, the two were temperamentally incompatible and as the years went by this became more and more obvious. Lord Grange was taken up with his career, his books, his garden and his religious devotions. His wife was volatile, unpredictable and increasingly jealous. She began to suspect that his visits to London were merely a cover for his liaisons with other women and she was obsessed with the notion that she would be supplanted.

Their differences erupted spectacularly in 1730 when Lord Grange's friends persuaded him to take his business affairs out of her hands and appoint a factor because her extravagance was ruining him. Lady Grange reacted violently. The public scenes and domestic crises she created convinced many people that she had become deranged, though her own relatives felt that she was deliberately feigning madness in order to gain sympathy. Whatever the truth of the matter, she was beside herself with jealousy and rage and her behaviour alienated even her own grown-up children.

Lord Grange's family and friends wrote frequent letters to him in London, detailing the outrageous tantrums of 'a certain person' and declaring that he would never be able to live with her again. The problem was, what could he do? His wife had not committed adultery and, far from deserting him, she was daily threatening to travel to London there to confront him publicly with her grievances. She would not heed a legal separation and when she began to claim that in addition to all his other alleged misdeeds he was plotting with the Jacobites, he grew desperate.

The solution he and his friends found for his difficulties has become notorious. In July 1732 Lady Grange was forcibly abducted from her house in Edinburgh and removed to the lonely island of Heiskir, off North Uist. Two years later she was transferred to St Kilda. There she remained, attended by a young girl and surrounded by people who spoke only Gaelic in her hearing. In 1738 her law agent received a letter purporting to come from her and he organised an expedition to rescue her, but by the time his ship arrived at St Kilda Lady Grange had been taken elsewhere. The last years of her life were spent in various places in Harris and Skye. She finally died in 1745, by then really deranged, and was buried at Trumpan in Waternish. Whatever the true cause of the discord between her husband and herself, they were each in their way the victims of the marriage laws of their time.

[SRO, Mar and Kellie Muniments, *passim*.]

Less spectacular than the marital problems of Lord and Lady Grange but equally well-known to contemporaries were the domestic difficulties of John, Earl of Lauderdale. Later raised by Charles II to the rank of Duke and given what amounted to vice-regal powers in Scotland, Lauderdale had been married at the age of fifteen to Lady Anna Home. Although they had only one child, a daughter, the marriage seems to have been reasonably successful for nearly forty years. During the Commonwealth period, when Lauderdale was imprisoned in the Tower of London, his wife visited him faithfully and when it was decided that he should be moved to even stricter confinement in Warwick Castle he was able to report, 'I bless God my wife prevailed to get the order recalled.'

After the Restoration they lived together at Highgate House in London, which Lady Anna had inherited from her mother. When Pepys visited them there in 1666 he found Lauderdale at supper with 'his Lady and some Scotch people'. The Earl

**37** Detail: James Erskine, Lord Grange, *c* 1714, attributed to William Aikman.
The Earl of Mar and Kellie: on loan to the Scottish National Portrait Gallery.

**38** Lady Anna Home, Countess of Lauderdale, *c*. 1665, by Sir Peter Lely.
Canvas: 49 × 40 inches (124.5 × 101.6 centimetres).
Hugo Morley-Fletcher Esq.

**39** John, 2nd Earl of Lauderdale, *c*. 1665, by Sir Peter Lely.
Canvas: 50 × 40 inches (127 × 101.6 centimetres).
Scottish National Portrait Gallery.

was still concerned enough for Lady Anna at that time to record that on receiving news of the death of her niece he 'sent immediately for my coach and came hither to comfort my poor wife, who is mightily afflicted for it.'

In later years Lady Anna suffered from constant ill-health and as time passed her husband became increasingly involved with Elizabeth Murray, Countess of Dysart. He had enjoyed apparently platonic friendships with a number of ladies in the past, but this was different. Elizabeth was fascinating, intelligent and dangerously ambitious. When her husband died in 1669 she made up her mind that she would supplant Lady Anna by whatever means possible. So successful was she in her campaign that by the following year relations between husband and wife were at their lowest ebb. Lady Anna retired to Paris, where Lauderdale rented a house for her, giving her a generous allowance on the understanding that she would never return. Indeed, she died there on 6 November 1671, sending her husband a last message regretting the coldness between them and forgiving him for his treatment of her.

[W C Mackenzie, *The Life and Times of John Maitland, Duke of Lauderdale* (London 1923), 307–9; Doreen Cripps, *Elizabeth of the Sealed Knot* (Kineton 1975), 42, 66, 76–7, 80, 89–90, 107.]

**40** Letter of Monsieur St Claude to John, 2nd Earl of Lauderdale, 1671.
National Library of Scotland, MS 14414 f3.
(Translated from the original French.)

[*November 1671*]

My Lord,
   It is most painful for me to be obliged to
make myself known to you on such a distressing occasion as this
which has made me write to you. God has been pleased to take back to himself Madame
The Countess of Lauderdale, the most excellent spouse He
had joined unto you, before dinner on Sunday the 6th of this month
when she died in my arms at half past eleven in the morning
after four days of most violent illness accompanied by
much suffering which I shall not describe to you. My Lord, the
singular edification which all our flock have received from her
during her stay in Paris, her piety, her goodness,
her humility, her wise and judicious conduct, her zeal for religion
and so many other admirable virtues those who had the honour
to be near her saw illuminated in her have filled our church
with veneration for her, and they will always hold her memory
in esteem. As I am one of those who had the advantage of
visiting her most often and since I assisted her
with my feeble consolations up until her last breath, she
had the kindness to choose me to send you her
last thoughts on your account. She therefore ordered me,
My Lord, to tell you that she died full of goodwill towards
you and greatly touched by the memory of the fondness you
once had for her whatever might be believed of the most
unhappy truth that your love had suffered an interruption
but that she bore no resentment either against
you or the cause of this coldness which she forgives
freely, begging you to hold her memory dear
after her death and praying God nevertheless to give you
His blessing . . .

In many cases of marital discord, family and
friends rallied round to try to effect a reconciliation.
When William, 9th Earl Marischal and his wife
Lady Mary Drummond separated after thirteen
years of marriage, her aunts and uncles were soon
discussing how to try to bring them together again.

*May it please Your Grace,*
*    The oblidging maner Your Grace was pleased to lay your comands on*
*My Lord Erroll and me to endeavor the continowance of peace and satisfaction*
*in the Earl Marischal's familie could not but add if possible to the inclination*
*wee formerly had of doing them all the service could lye in our power and what I*
*consider as my duty to Your Grace in aquainting you with what hes hapened since made*
*me resolv on being trublsome rather then omit to doe it, which though it be not so*
*well as their friends does wish, yet at the desire of some of her relations and*
*assurance it would be acceptable to Your Grace, she hes condescended to pass from*
*some part of her first resolution and hes now said that after a while's absence*
*and convincing evidence that he continows to love or faver her she will again*
*return to his company, which to part with is the nixt worst truble she could*
*suffer to th[e] fear she seems to be in or being again unkyndly used, but I hope Your*
*Grace and other friends will prevail with to overcome those apprehensions which*
*occasions her unwilingness to a present complyance and the Earl is now so inclinable*
*to doe everything that may satisfie her that I hope a litl time will take off all*
*to a comfortable living together which all that wishes any of them*
*realy well canot but see to be both in the intrest of themselves and their children*
*who are so very beautifull and hes so great a share of all the advantages*
*thir years are capable of that it is impossible to see them and not admire*
*them, and a seperat living does also threaten other inconveniencys that I am*
*unwiling to name and none can think of without regrate that hes any concern*
*for that nobl family's prosperity, but I hope may yet be retrived be her good conduct*
*and his complyance with the advice of his friends and relations . . .*

**41** Letter of Anne, Countess of Erroll to James, 4th
Duke of Hamilton, 1703.
Hamilton Archives, C1/5079.

Some couples separated irrevocably, some were reconciled and a few passed their married lives in a state of perpetual warfare, apparently thriving on their differences. Such was the case of Sophia Clerk and her husband Gabriel Little. Almost from the time of their elopement Sophia was bombarding her own family with complaints about her husband's unreasonable behaviour, nor was he silent about her faults. One moment Sophia would declare that she was leaving Gabriel for good, and the next she would declare her undying affection for him. After a separation in 1718 Gabriel wrote a dignified letter to his father-in-law declaring that he would not have his wife back, but a few weeks later they were once more enthusiastically resuming their old arguments.

*Honoured Sir,*

*After mature deliberation and advising with friends,*
*my resolution is that your daughter, my wife, should not come home*
*to me again in regard her humour is so cross and inclinations so*
*vicious and everything about her so unfit for cohabitation that it*
*will render both her life and mine uneasie and uncomfortable in this*
*world and it will likewayes tend more to the glory of God our being*
*seperat than together. Bot that shee may not be any wayes destitut*
*or troublesome to any of her own or my relationes, I am content*
*to allow her ane yearly aliment which can be bot small, considering*
*the other joynture, the mentinance of myself and children and debts*
*quhich I'm obliged to pay.*

*Sir, you may be sure this resolution is both burdensome and grievous*
*to me. If it could be helped otherwayes, I am shortly to go from*
*town and cannot expect to see you again at this tyme, bot I heartily*
*pray the Lord may strengthen you under the present trouble and*
*may give you a perfect recovery in his due time. I shall still retain*
*that filial regard for you as formerly and am,*

*Honoured Sir,*
*Your most affectionat son and humble servant,*
*Gabriel Little.*

*Edinburgh    21 October*
*1718*

**42** Letter of Gabriel Little to his father-in-law, Sir John Clerk of Penicuik, 1718.
SRO, Clerk of Penicuik Papers, GD 18/5250/40.

**43** The Henwife of Castle Grant, 17[2]6, by Richard
Waitt.
(Wrongly inscribed 1706.)
Canvas: 30 × 25 inches (76.2 × 63.5 centimetres).
The Earl of Seafield.

# 4

# Activities

By law, a wife's 'natural and proper province' was the domestic sphere and indeed her circumstances were bound to limit her activities. For many women the child-bearing years were spent in a succession of pregnancies so that for long periods at a time travel on horseback or by jolting coach was too dangerous, not to mention too uncomfortable. Yet it would be wrong to suppose that the women of the seventeenth and eighteenth centuries spent their lives passively at home, engaged in household chores or whiling away their leisure as best they could. On the contrary, they undertook a surprisingly wide range of activities.

Much, of course, depended upon the individual's place in society. The great lady obviously had more scope for her activities than did her less well-placed contemporaries. Very often she would find herself undertaking responsibilities which in theory belonged to her husband. After 1603 the Court was in London and so men of rank and position made an annual trip south, spending months at a time away from home. Usually their wives and mothers were left behind to administer their property for them, legally constituted to do so. In 1684, for example, Sir John Dick had to be out of Scotland for several weeks so before he went he had his lawyers draw up a document narrating that he, 'being verie confident and haveing the experience of the fidelitie of Dam[e] Anna Patersone my beloved spouse and of her good governement and ardent desyre to promove my interest', appoints her his 'actrix, factrix and special errand bearer and plenipotentiarie' empowered to uplift his revenues and generally to run his estate on his behalf.

Charity and religion had always been areas in which ladies interested themselves and many took an active part in promoting local industry and education. Correspondence of the time shows that they certainly did not lack strong opinions about current political affairs so although they could usually take no direct action they undoubtedly influenced their husbands to a varying extent.

Of course, at other levels of society economic necessity compelled women to seek employment outside the home. Many young girls found work before marriage as domestic servants. In the great Scottish houses of the seventeenth and early eighteenth centuries the staff was predominantly male: there was an army of footmen, grooms, cooks and so forth with one or two women employed as chambermaids, washerwomen, nurses and hen-wives. These were often the wives of the male servants. Many other smaller households had a living-in servant, though, who was frequently a relative. Shopkeepers, professional men, tradesmen and tenant farmers alike all had their servant maids.

Again, shopkeepers and tradesmen had the assistance of their wives in the running of their businesses. This is borne out by the large number of widows who carried on the businesses after their husbands' death and obviously had the experience to do so successfully. As time passed, too, women found that a number of new careers were open to them. The eighteenth century saw the establishment of female milliners, dressmakers and teachers, usually unmarried and earning their own living independently of their families.

**44** Lady Grisel Baillie, 1717, by William Aikman.
Canvas: 30 × 25 inches (76.2 × 63.5 centimetres).
The Earl of Haddington KT MC.

One lady rightly famed for her household management was Lady Grisel Baillie, eldest daughter of Sir Patrick Hume. Her responsibilities had begun early in life. As the celebrated story recounts, it was Grisel who stole out by night to carry food to her father when he lay hidden in the vaults of Polwarth parish church, evading arrest for alleged complicity in the Rye House Plot. When he and his family later escaped to the continent it was Grisel who took over the running of the household from her invalid mother.

With the Revolution of 1688 the Humes were able to return to Britain and Grisel became the wife of George Baillie of Marchmont. Taking her domestic duties very seriously, she attended cookery lessons given by a Mr Addison and with meticulous care she kept all the family accounts. She noted her expenditure in precise detail in a series of ledgers which exist to this day and on one occasion she sat up late for several weeks putting her father's financial papers in order.

During more than fifty years of married life George Baillie entrusted her with the entire administration of his finances, 'without scarce asking a question about them, except sometimes to say to her "Is my debt paid yet?" though often did she apply to him for direction and advice.' She brought up her children with loving care and in the midst of her domestic concerns had time to compose a number of well known Scottish songs. She died on 6 December 1746 at the age of eighty and was buried with her husband at Mellerstain.

[*The Household Book of Lady Grisel Bailie* ed. Robert Scott-Moncrieff (Scottish History Society 1911.]

In the winter of 1713–14 Lady Grisel Baillie's husband ordered from Colin Mackenzie the Edinburgh goldsmith this coffee pot and hot milk jug, engraved with his arms. Lady Grisel recorded the purchase in her household book for January 1714, noting that the price of having the two pieces made was £6:8:3.

**45** Lady Grisel Baillie's coffee pot and hot milk jug, 1713.
National Museum of Antiquities of Scotland, MEQ 899–900.

One of the oldest established domestic activities was spinning. The mistress of the house either undertook this herself or employed women to do it under her supervision. Spinning wheels had been introduced into Scotland during the Middle Ages but the technique shown in David Allan's drawing remained popular throughout the seventeenth and eighteenth centuries. The girl is using a distaff round which are wound the prepared fibres of wool or flax. It is supported against her left shoulder and its end is presumably tucked into her apron strings. From her right hand is suspended the weighted spindle.

[Information from Mrs Helen Bennett, National Museum of Antiquities of Scotland.]

**46** A Scotch Maid, *c.* 1782, by David Allan.
Pen and wash: $9\frac{1}{4} \times 7\frac{1}{8}$ inches ($23.5 \times 18.1$ centimetres).
National Gallery of Scotland, Department of Prints and Drawings.

**47** Letter of the Dowager Countess of Mar to her son,
Lord Grange, 1707.
SRO, Mar and Kellie Muniments, GD 124/15/552/3.

Another important feminine preoccupation was
the servant problem, though few ladies had to
cope with such dramatic difficulties as did the
Dowager Countess of Mar. Her home was in
Stirling Castle, her eldest son being the Hereditary
Keeper, and life was complicated by the presence
of a garrison. The tragic episode in May 1707 was
nothing to do with the soldiers, though, but
resulted from friction between the domestic
servants.

*My D[ear] C[hild],*
*I trust and pray that this solemn occassion*
*[a communion service, probably] may be bless'd*
*to you and your wife and it's refreshing to me to know that*
*you have been minding that great business which is sure the one*
*thing necessarie for when all sublunary and created com-*
*forts fails then those whose minds are steayd on Him*
*will have perfect peace. Let me know how your wife is after*
*her being out and I will be far from misconstructing her not*
*wryting. I hope you got my letter which I did wryt upon*
*Fryday with one inclos'd to your brother M[ar] which I'm concerned*
*to have quickly and save [ie safe] to him. Now, dear James, I'm*
*to show you an unluckie thing that is fallen out in our*
*familie upon Saturday last after dinnir. The cook's man*
*was coming by the coachman and had been baking and rub'd*
*his cloathes upon the coachman's black cloathes, so he*
*gave him a thrust and then some ill words past betwixt*
*them and they fell to blows, so some of the servants and sojers [of the garrison]*
*did take hold of S. Calander because he was a*
*strong young fellow and the cook's man was old and weak*
*so in the time they were holding him he kicked with*
*his foot the other poor creature in the low part of*
*his bellie, so in a verie litile he cry'd out with pain, but*
*the servants thought it would go over and did not tell me*
*of it till Sabath morning. However, that same night*
*and morning H. Chrystie gave him some things and let blood*
*of him, so when I came from church I found he was*
*dead a verie litile before I came in, so you may easilie*
*judge how heavie it was to me that God had permit'd*
*so sad an accident.*
*Stirling Castle   20 May 1707*

**48** Dame Janet Dick's Poem
SRO, Dick-Cunynghame of Prestonfield Muniments,
GD 331/5/1.

The domestic arrangements for guests naturally came within the women's province. One lady famed for her hospitality at Prestonfield was Dame Janet Dick (see Section 2). Not only did she entertain a wide circle of guests including Allan Ramsay the portrait painter and Benjamin Franklin, but she was able to join in the elder Ramsay's game of sending verse epistles and composed a long poem excusing her absence from Edinburgh and inviting him to dine.

*Dear Allan, thanks to you and muse*
*Comes from myself and Knight my spouse*
*For your kind, canty, cosh epistle*
*It warm'd my heart and made me whistle*
*In spite of gloomy, gloury weather*
*It made my soul as light as feather*
*Clapt hold of paper, pen and ink*
*To try my hand if rhime cow'd [ie could] clink*
*To tell you fairly my best reason*
*For being country muse this season*
*Was not that I had ought aversion*
*For city pastimes and deversions*
*But that I have no mind to steal*
*And send poor tradesfolks to the Deil*
*Take aff braw cleaths till goud in purse*
*Can save me mony a heavy curse*
*From Castlehill to Netherbow*
*Where folks most run the gauntlet now*
*Who run in debt to all they meet*
*And hear there grumbling on the street*
*But ready money when it comes*
*Will makes us all rise from our bums*
*With haste to spread the blessing round*
*That is with honest plenty crown'd*
*The winds may goul, the floods may flow*
*But peace of mind the[y] ever know*
*Wha from contentment know true blis*
*And envy no man what is his,*
*Dispise the luxry of the towns*
*More upright beaus than downright clowns*
*Admire ald farant [old-fashioned] common sense*
*Which country air and words despence*
*But now I see the blooming spring*
*I see, I feel it on the wing*
*Haste, balmie gales and April shours*

*And deck my filds with all your flours*
*Mien time dear Allan, know a goose*
*Well feed and roasted in the juice*
*With onions, peper, time and sage*
*In honour of the last year's stage*
*Is sacrifis'd on Thursday next,*
*The parson com's, the hour is fixd*
*Then let us droun all care in claret*
*My Knight expects you winna spare it.*

**49** Anne, 3rd Duchess of Hamilton, 1679, by Sir Godfrey Kneller.
Canvas: 55 × 43 inches (139.8 × 109.2 centimetres).
The Duke of Hamilton.

The wide range of activities possible for a woman of influence is well illustrated in the career of Anne, 3rd Duchess of Hamilton. When her father was executed as a supporter of Charles I and her uncle died from wounds received fighting for Charles II, Anne became Duchess in her own right. Her inheritance was, however, sadly depleted. Most of her estates had been confiscated by the Cromwellian government and there were huge debts left by both her father and grandfather. Although only nineteen, Duchess Anne resolved that she would rescue the family fortunes and devoted the rest of her long life to doing precisely this.

She began by choosing as her husband William Douglas, Earl of Selkirk. He was two years her junior, a younger son of the Marquis of Douglas and a Roman Catholic. Duchess Anne had inherited her estates on the strict condition that she should marry a Presbyterian, so the Earl renounced his religion in order to become her husband. Apart from her deep affection for him, she saw in him the financial abilities she needed to help her in her task and indeed their partnership was to be a most successful one. Duchess Anne bore him thirteen children and together they worked for the repossession of the Hamilton estates. Gradually they paid off debts and fines, reclaimed the lands and gathered money for the improvement of their property. With the Restoration, Charles II created her husband the Duke of Hamilton, at Duchess Anne's request.

Although she was recognised as head of her family, the Duchess could not sit in parliament or privy council because she was a woman but her correspondence makes it plain that she took a keen interest in all the leading issues of her day. She always declared that she was above party politics or religious faction and indeed it is notable that in an era when her fellow Covenanters were persecuting Quakers, she gave them her protection. Even so, such were her abilities that the Presbyterian ministers looked to her for advice and when Union with England was proposed, so wrong did she feel that the move would be for Scotland that she took an active part in raising opposition. Economic affairs attracted her attention too, and she subscribed generously to funds set up to establish the Bank of Scotland and the ill-fated trading colony at Darien.

Nearest to her heart, however, was the presentation and improvement of her own estates. She saw her inheritance as a sacred trust, and the welfare of her tenants as her main concern. Confessing to her family that she was no housewife, she left the domestic running of her household largely to her servants and gave her mind instead to larger matters. Under her supervision a new Hamilton Palace rose up in place of the old, trees were planted and gardens extended. Her husband died in 1694 but she carried out the plans they had made together. In the burgh of Hamilton itself she built a new school and almshouse, established a spinning school to train the local girls, provided scholarships to the Merchant Maiden Hospital in Edinburgh, set up a woollen manufactory and encouraged lace-making. Under her patronage Bo'ness was granted its founding charter and became a thriving port. Strathaven was provided with a new schoolhouse and waulkmill. To Arran she sent a doctor, a catechist and an 'ambulatory schoolmaster'. She introduced coal mining and saltmaking there, set up a harbour and village at Lamlash, provided the island with a ferryboat and built a chapel at Lochranza. Instances of her charity to individuals were numerous and it is not surprising that she was known throughout the west of Scotland as 'Good Duchess Anne'.

[Rosalind K Marshall, *The Days of Duchess Anne* (London, 1973).]

**50** Henrietta, Duchess of Gordon, *c.* 1750, attributed to Philippe Mercier.
Canvas: 50 × 40 inches (127 × 101.6 centimetres).
The Earl of Wemyss and March KT LLD.

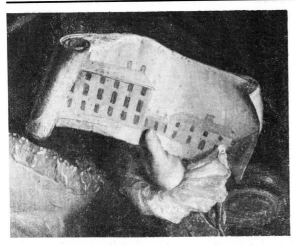

**51** Detail of portrait of Henrietta, Duchess of Gordon: plan of Prestonhall, Midlothian.

**52** William Adam's plan for Prestonhall, commissioned by the Duchess.
(Plate 108, *Vitruvius Scoticus*)
Photograph by the Royal Commission on Ancient Monuments, Scotland, MLD 86/1.

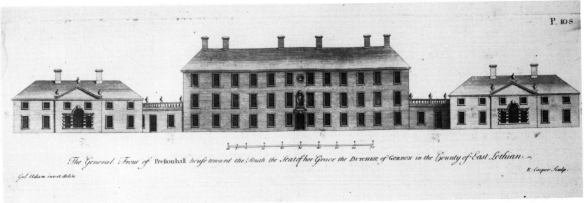

P. 108

*The General Front of Prestonhall house toward the South the Seat of her Grace the Dvchess of Gordon in the County of East Lothian.*

*Gul. Adam inv. et delin.*                                                                                               *R. Cooper Sculp.*

Building was an interest which often preoccupied the women of the family. The determined-looking lady seated with a plan in her hand is Henrietta Mordaunt, Duchess of Gordon. English by birth, she married the Duke of Gordon in 1707 and took an energetic interest in his affairs. Having been with the Jacobite army of 1715, the Duke was imprisoned in Edinburgh Castle for a time, then lived a retired life until his death in 1728. The Duchess, left with a family of five sons and seven daughters, brought them up according to her own ideas. Although the Gordons were staunchly Catholic she raised her children in the Protestant faith, thereby earning the gratitude of the General Assembly of the Church of Scotland, who sent her a special letter of thanks in 1730. Five years later the government presented her with a pension of £1,000 a year but this was withdrawn in 1745 after she set out a breakfast by the roadside for Prince Charles Edward when he passed her gates.

She took particular interest in agricultural affairs and the story goes that she brought English ploughs and ploughmen to the north to work on her son's estates. In about 1738 the Duchess went to live at Prestonhall, near Dalkeith with her younger children. Dissatisfied with the old house, she commissioned William Adam to design a new, larger mansion for the site and it is his plan which she holds in her right hand.

**53** Helen Hope, Countess of Haddington, 1694, by Sir John Medina.
Canvas: $48\frac{1}{2} \times 39\frac{1}{2}$ inches ($123.2 \times 100.3$ centimetres).
The Earl of Haddington KT MC.

By the end of the seventeenth century planting had become a fashionable occupation for landowners, and it was one in which their wives frequently shared. Agricultural improvements were well under way by now and trees not only protected fields but beautified an estate. One lady who was well aware of the advantages was Helen Hope, sister of the 1st Earl of Hopetoun.

At the age of eighteen, in 1696, Helen married her cousin Thomas, 6th Earl of Haddington. Their first years together were spent at Leslie House in Fife but in 1700 they moved to the family home at Tyninghame, in East Lothian. The estate there had been let out for some years to careless tenants who had neglected it sadly and in particular there were very few trees. When questioned about this, the local people replied that there was no point in planting young saplings, for the salt sea air and the cold east winds would surely destroy them. By his own account, the Earl would have left the situation as it was. Writing a description of his activities for the benefit of his grandchildren, he was later to confess, 'I took pleasure in sports, dogs and horses but had no manner of inclination to plant, inclose or improve my grounds.' His wife, however, was of a different disposition. 'But as your grandmother was a great lover of planting', he continued, 'she did what she could to engage me to it, but in vain. At last she asked leave to go about it, which she did, and I was much pleased with some little things that were both well laid out and executed, though none of them are now to be seen, for when the designs grew more extensive we were forced to take away what first was done.'

His interest caught, the Earl gradually forgot his horses and dogs. He decided that he himself would lay out a fashionable 'wilderness'. No sooner had this been done than his Countess came to him with another proposal. She announced that she would like to enclose the Muir of Tyninghame, a piece of rough ground extending to more than 300 acres Scots. The Earl was doubtful. 'It seemed too great an attempt and almost everybody advised her not to undertake it as being impracticable, of which number I confess I was one. But she said if I would agree to it she made no doubt of getting it finished. I gave her free leave.' Indeed, he soon found that he himself was planning out walks through the plantation on the Muir and when he and his wife differed on the proposed central point they called in three friends to act as arbitrators. Eventually 'an incredible number of trees was planted' on what had been a stretch of barren waste and the Countess renamed the area Binning Wood.

By this time even their ten year old son shared their enthusiasm and the Earl was reading every available work about the cultivation of trees. He became renowned throughout the country for his planting activities and himself wrote a learned treatise on the subject. He never failed to pay tribute to his Countess who had started it all. Her part was summed up by a fellow improver in his great work which he engagingly entitled *An Essay on the Dry Rot*. Writing of the Countess he said:

*'Thus can good wives, when wise, in every station*
*On man work miracles of reformation*
*And were such wives more common, their husbands would*
*                                        endure it*

*However great the malady, a loving wife can cure it,*
*And much their aid is wanted, we hope they'll use it*
*                                        fairish,*
*While [ie until] barren ground, where wood should be,*
*                        appears in every parish.'*

[Thomas, 6th Earl of Haddington, *Treatise on the manner of raising Forest Trees* (1761 edition); Sir William Fraser, *Memorials of the Earls of Haddington* (Edinburgh 1889), i, 239–61.]

**54** Margaret, Duchess of Douglas, *c.* 1760, by an unknown artist.
Canvas: 30 × 25 inches (76.2 × 63.5 centimetres).
Mrs A V C Douglas of Mains.

One of the most celebrated lawsuits in Scottish history involved two female protagonists. This was the Douglas Cause, a protracted legal battle which raged for more than ten years between the House of Douglas and the House of Hamilton. All the eminent lawyers of the day were employed, hundreds of witnesses were heard, thousands of pages of evidence were produced and such was the public interest that crowds rioted in the streets when a verdict was finally reached.

The point at issue was who should succeed to the Douglas estates when the old Duke died. He had married late in life and had no children. His sister, Lady Jane Douglas, had likewise remained unmarried for many years until, when she was nearly fifty, she eloped to France with Colonel John Steuart, an impoverished military man. To the astonishment of everyone she then announced that she had given birth to twins. One baby died but the other, Archibald, would succeed to his uncle's estates if he were truly Lady Jane's legitimate son. If not, the inheritance would pass to the young Duke of Hamilton.

55 Elizabeth Gunning, c. 1752, by Gavin Hamilton. Canvas: 26⅝ × 21⅞ inches (67.5 × 55.5 centimetres). Scottish National Portrait Gallery.

The leading contenders in the ensuing struggle were Elizabeth Gunning, the mother of Hamilton and Margaret Douglas, the old Duke of Douglas's wife. In character and in appearance these two ladies were very different. Elizabeth was one of the beautiful Irish Gunning sisters who had taken London by storm in the early 1750s. She so enchanted James, 6th Duke of Hamilton that, ignoring his family's disapproval, he married her at midnight on St Valentine's Day 1752 in a secret ceremony with a bed curtain ring doing service as a wedding ring. His family's disapproval faded when he brought Elizabeth back to Scotland. Her beauty, her charm and her dignified manner won her great popularity. She became the centre of Scottish society, interested herself in local affairs and bore her husband two sons and a daughter before his early death in 1758. A year afterwards she married Colonel John Campbell, later 4th Duke of Argyll. By him she had three more sons and two daughters, but her main preoccupation was that her eldest son should succeed to the Douglas estates.

Her opponent, Duchess Peggy as she was known to all, was equally determined that they should go to Archibald Douglas. Shrewd, famous for her outspoken wit and high spirits, and certainly no beauty, she remained unmarried for many years. She came from the Lanarkshire family of Douglas of Mains and when a friend teased her about being an old maid, she retorted jokingly that she would never marry unless she could be Duchess of Douglas. Her words were prophetic. According to tradition, she visited Douglas Castle twelve years later to persuade the Duke to secure for her nephew an army commission. She told him in her forthright way that he needed a wife, and on 28 February 1758 she drove up to the Castle in a hired chaise to marry him. She was forty-four.

Her struggle against the Hamiltons began almost at once. Although she had never met the Duke's sister, who was by now dead, she was convinced that Archibald was Lady Jane's legitimate son. She involved herself vigorously on his behalf and redoubled her efforts when her husband died in 1761. Both she and Elizabeth Gunning visited France in separate attempts to find evidence supporting their own contentions. The Hamiltons declared that Lady Jane had acquired two babies from French mothers and had passed them off as her own. Duchess Peggy was adamant that Archibald was a genuine Douglas. Not until the summer of 1767 did the Court of Session give its verdict in favour of the Duke of Hamilton. There was an immediate public outcry and, not to be defeated, the Douglases appealed to the House of Lords. After a dramatic debate the Lords reversed the decision and found that Archibald was the true heir. Because he was inheriting through his mother, he could not succeed to the title of Duke of Douglas but the estates were now legally his.

Duchess Peggy survived to enjoy her triumph for another seven years. Elizabeth Gunning lost her eldest son soon after the House of Lords decision. She concealed her sorrow and disappointment as best she could and remained an admired figure in society until her death in 1790.

[Horace Bleackley, *The Story of a Beautiful Duchess* (London 1908).]

Upon occasion, a woman's role of generally overseeing the family estates on behalf of an absent husband or son could involve her actively in public business. This was especially true of those women whose husbands participated in the Jacobite Risings of 1715 and 1745. With men killed in battle, executed or exiled, wives were left to remedy the situation as best they could.

Lady Margaret Hamilton, Countess of Panmure was certainly equal to the challenge. The youngest daughter of Scotland's leading nobleman, the Duke of Hamilton, she married the Episcopalian Earl of Panmure in 1687. Her Presbyterian family disapproved somewhat of the match, but it proved to be a happy and successful one. The Earl was wealthy, his house at Panmure in Angus was luxurious and their only sorrow in the early years was that the Countess was childless.

With the events of 1715, the settled pattern of their lives was permanently disrupted. An ardent supporter of the Stewart cause, the Earl joined the Jacobite forces, was wounded at the battle of Sheriffmuir and was only rescued from enemy hands by the intervention of his brother Harry. Shortly afterwards, he fled to France. Parliament thereupon attainted him for high treason and his estates were forfeited to the crown.

In spite of her desire to join him abroad, the Countess remained behind at Panmure determined, as she put it, 'to hold the grip as long as I can.' For the next few years she was to devote all her indefatigable energies to the attempt to regain the estates for her husband and his family. She wrote literally hundreds of letters trying to persuade people to speak on behalf of the Earl. She consulted lawyers in Edinburgh and she went to London no fewer than four times between the spring of 1717 and the autumn of 1720, spending endless hours negotiating with the influential men of the day. She kept her husband supplied not only with cheerful news but with sums of money, investing some of their precious funds in South Sea Stock in a vain attempt to increase their resources.

In the end, her efforts to buy back some of the lands from the government failed, but she did manage to lease Panmure House and the surrounding policies from the purchasers, the York Buildings Company. After three years of separation she visited her husband in France and then made regular journeys to the continent to see him. He died in Paris in 1723. His Countess spent the remainder of her life in Scotland, a leading figure in Edinburgh society until her death on 6 December 1731.

**56** Lady Margaret Hamilton, Countess of Panmure, *c.* 1701, by Sir John Medina.
Canvas: 60 × 54 inches (152.4 × 137.1 centimetres).
The Earl of Dalhousie KT GBE MC.

Panmure 22 February 1716

My Dearest Heart,

    I had yours on Thursday last. You may be sure that
I was exstreamlie glade to know you had so pro[s]perous a voyage.
Bles'd be God that he delivered you out of the hand of your enne-
mies. I trust in His mercie that He will on[e] time or other deliver us out of
the heavie trouble we are att present under. I shall long till I
hear againe from you, but not knowing how this may come to
your hand I dar[e] venture to writ very litle. I have desir'd a friend
to send you a letter of credit which I hope he will however if
tho it should be long acomming I hope you shall be in no strait
in the meantime. You may be sure I have a melancholy time on't
here but I resolve to hold by the grip as long as I can and when I
consider that others are yet in worse circumstances having their
husbands now condemn'd to a sad sentence att London (which you'l see by the news
papers) I think I ought to submitt the more willinglie to my trouble.
I have writ to several friends in your behalf but I'm affraid it's not
in the power of any Scotts man to do for us. God Allmighty look to our
distress and turn the hearts of our enemies to us. This poor countrey
is in a sad condition by the march of the army, so gett our
estates who will, they will not be much the richer of
them for some time. The Duke of Argyll is not yet returnd from the north but
is expected att Montrose this night in his way to Edinburgh. Several of our
people has surrendered themselves to him, particularlie Poorie and I
hear a frind of yours designes to do the same, he you saw that afternoon
before you left Dundee. Whither this course be advisable or not time
must trye, but I hope in God you are better where you are . . .
. . . I send this letter att a venture
so shall add no more but that it's thought fitte you live very
privatelie and keep no correspondence with a certain court. God
Almighty preserve and support you under your trouble. So Adieu
My Dearest Heart.
I hope the wound in your head is
now quite well, which pray lett me
know the first time you writ. I
hope your honest friend that is with
you is well. I often wish I were also
with you but I must have patience the
best way I can, tho I find it's a hard
precept.

The best known women of any era are probably those who played a romantic role in public affairs. The Jacobite ladies are particularly remembered for their courage and most notable of them, of course, was Flora Macdonald. Orphaned at an early age, Flora was brought up in the Hebrides, on the island of South Uist. Lady Macdonald, the wife of Sir Alexander Macdonald of the Isles, took an interest in her and, admiring her accomplished singing and playing of the spinet, sent her to school in Edinburgh to finish her education. She spent several years in the city, accompanying the Macdonalds home each summer.

It was during a visit to Benbecula with them that Flora was persuaded to help Prince Charles Edward Stewart. Fleeing from the Hanoverians after his defeat at Culloden, the Prince went into hiding in the north west of Scotland. His companions thought it best that he should seek refuge in Skye for a short time and so evolved the plan that he should disguise himself as Flora's female servant, Betty Burke. Flora was at first reluctant to take part in the scheme but, giving way to persuasion, she safely escorted the Prince across to Skye, thereby making a permanent place for herself in Scottish history and legend.

Her part in his escape did not go unnoticed by the authorities. She was arrested, taken by sea to London and imprisoned in the Tower for a short time. The Act of Indemnity of 1747 liberated her and she remained in the south for some months, a popular and fêted member of society. It was during this period that Richard Wilson painted the portrait Flora presented to the captain of the ship which had brought her south.

On her return to Scotland she married a local farmer, Allan Macdonald. They had five sons and two daughters. Eventually they emigrated to North Carolina, only to be involved in the Civil War there. Her husband was appointed Brigadier General and Flora accompanied him on his campaigns until he was captured. After considerable hardship she returned safely to Scotland where they were at last reunited. Flora died at Kingsburgh on 5 March 1790.

**58** Flora Macdonald, 1747, by Richard Wilson.
Canvas: 30⅛ × 23⅛ inches (76.4 × 58.6 centimetres). Scottish National Portrait Gallery.

**59** Anne Smith, Mrs Thomas Ruddiman, 1749, by William Denune.
Canvas: 30 × 25 inches (76.2 × 63.5 centimetres).
Scottish National Portrait Gallery.

The daring adventures of the Jacobite ladies have been remembered while their less spectacular but equally resourceful sisters are often forgotten. It is not usual to find portraits or biographies of the ordinary women who determinedly made their living in adverse circumstances but the evidence suggests that a surprising number did pursue careers of their own. In both Scotland and England, for example, it was quite usual to find women running printers' businesses. Of course the ladies concerned were widows of the original printers and how far they participated in the business varied. The best known of all was Agnes Campbell

(Number 60), but equally resolute was Anne Smith, the third wife of Thomas Ruddiman. Herself the daughter of an Edinburgh woollen draper, she carried on her husband's publishing activities after his death in 1757. Amidst strong competition she continued to produce the highly successful *Rudiments of the Latin Tongue* for which he had obtained a monopoly the year before his death. Other firms were anxious to share in the sales of this popular work and in 1758 one competitor actually produced an illegal edition of it. Mrs Ruddiman was equal to him, however. She threatened with such effect to sue him that he meekly handed over to her all the copies he had printed. Ten years later she was producing a seventeenth edition, running to no fewer than 20,000 copies.

Mrs Ruddiman died in October 1769 and was buried beside her husband in Greyfriars Churchyard, Edinburgh.

Proudly styling herself 'His Majesty's Printress', Mrs Agnes Anderson determinedly carried on her late husband's business in Edinburgh, thereby arousing what can only be described as the venomous hatred of her masculine competitors. The books she produced were much criticised by them for the poor quality of the printing, but in fact the works emanating from her presses were no worse than the other material produced elsewhere in Scotland at the time. Waging vigorous warfare with her rivals, she continued to enjoy the monopoly of producing certain official publications and something of her other business activities is seen in a letter she sent to Baron Clerk in 1711.

**60** Letter of Mrs Agnes Anderson to Baron Clerk, 1711.
SRO, Clerk of Penicuik Papers, GD 18/5278/6.

*Edinburgh    September 4th 1711*

*Sir,*

*Yours of the 31 last month I re-
ceived, wherein ye give me an account of two requests ye make not
in your own behalf, but Mr McGeorge's. The first is that he should
have a pass key to the fountain at Pennicok, which I am very willing
to grant, and desires he may cause make one there if possibly it can be done
and keep it allannerly [ie only] for his own use. The second request, which was
that he should have as much paper as he might write his sermons
upon, I am as willing to grant as the former, so entreats he may acquiant
me what sort of paper he would have and what quantity, and it shall
be readily sent him, for I am very sensible of his great care of
and his good service done to my men there, and I heartily wish they
may improve aright his most edifying doctrine. You may be assured
that I account it my great honour to be capable to serve you or him
on your account, and if requir'd, I shall do it to the outmost of my
power. According to your desire I have sent you a ream of paper
of the same size with your inclosed before it was cut, and also with the
same mark and of equal fineness, with which I am hopeful Your
Honour will be pleased. This with my humble duty to your kind
lady and all the rest of your honourable family is all at present from*
*Sir, your humble and very much*
*obliged servitrix,*
*Agnes Campbell.*

[Only the signature is in Mrs Anderson's own writing].

**61** An Edinburgh Fishwife, *c.* 1780, by David Allan.
Pen and watercolour, $9\frac{3}{4} \times 7\frac{3}{8}$ inches (24.7 × 18.7 centimetres).
National Gallery of Scotland, Department of Prints and Drawings.

**62** An Edinburgh Lace Woman with a Distaff, 1784, by David Allan.
Pen and watercolour, $6\frac{1}{4} \times 4\frac{3}{4}$ inches (15.9 × 12.00 centimetres).
National Gallery of Scotland, Department of Prints and Drawings.

Many of the shopkeepers and street vendors were women. Perhaps the only one of the latter familiar to us to-day is the fishwife in her traditional costume, drawn by David Allan about 1780. His Lace Woman is an intriguing figure. She sold trimmings for clothing and here she displays her braids and laces by having them suspended from a long staff. In her other hand she holds a packet of laces.

In the seventeenth and eighteenth centuries an increasing number of women were finding themselves employment as teachers and midwives. Usually, however, the professions were not open to them, in part because of their lack of education. Occasionally there was a girl of such promise that she could make a career as a writer or, even more rarely, as a professional artist. One such was Anne Forbes, the granddaughter of William Aikman the portrait painter. So promising was Anne that in 1767 a group of patrons sent her to study in Rome accompanied by her mother, who acted as chaperone. She spent three years in Italy working with Gavin Hamilton, a fellow-Scot, who observed that 'she has great talents as well as a love for her profession and her industry is equal to her genius'.

In 1771 Anne moved to London where she hoped to establish herself as a portrait painter, but she discovered to her disappointment that her style was not fashionable and that she had too many rivals. She therefore returned to Edinburgh where she set up in George Square as a drawing teacher, obtaining commissions for portraits in pastel and oils whenever she could.

[David and Francina Irwin, *Scottish Painters at Home and Abroad 1700–1900* (London 1975), 76–7.]

**63** Anne Forbes, 1781, by David Allan.
Canvas: 15⅛ × 12⅝ inches (38.3 × 32 centimetres).
Scottish National Portrait Gallery.

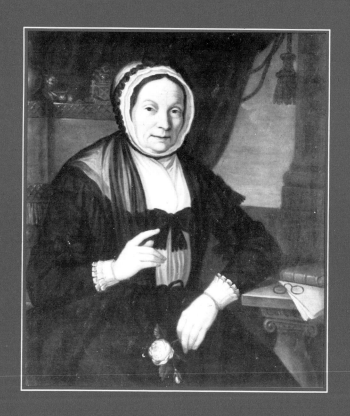

# 5

# Widows

When a leading man of the day died, his widow dressed herself and her family in black, hung her rooms with black, sealed her letters with black wax and devoted the weeks immediately after his death to the ritual of mourning. Her own way of life altered from that moment. Her marriage contract had, of course, provided for this contingency. She would now maintain herself on the jointure, those lands allocated to her by her husband's family in the contract. She would draw revenues in the form of rents and she would sell or use in her household those rents paid to her in kind. She would also be provided with accommodation—a dower house or its equivalent—though she might choose not to live in it. She might stay on in the family home to run it for her son or she might occupy apartments in his establishment.

For lesser members of society the position varied considerably. The well-to-do had their marriage contracts and so provision was made for them. A merchant's widow could be comfortably settled, drawing revenues from his property. A tradesman's widow could occupy quarters in her son's house. A shopkeeper's wife might inherit his business when he died. Many women, of course, did not have marriage contracts. Instead, by law, they were entitled to the liferent from a third of the husband's heritage and a third of his moveable estate (half if they had no children).

Such were the legal safeguards but the trouble was that a woman all too often found herself left with debts and no income when her husband died. Economic necessity therefore forced her to seek employment. The only alternative was to hope for assistance from relatives or to exist on a tiny sum paid out in the burghs to 'the town poor'. Lists of the latter invariably include the names of widows unable to work.

Nor were the difficulties which beset them entirely financial. The procession of widows coming to the Privy Council with complaints of being harried, oppressed and even attacked by relatives and neighbours indicates how ready people were to take advantage of the widow's unprotected state. It is not surprising that many tried to solve their financial difficulties by remarrying. A widow had full control of her choice of a second husband. There was now no question of bowing to parental authority. Remarriage therefore seemed to many to be the most sensible solution to their problems.

**64** Catherine Bruce, Lady Bruce of Clackmannan, *c.* 1779, by an unknown artist.
Canvas: 36⅛ × 28⅛ inches (91.7 × 71.4 centimetres).
The Earl and Countess of Airlie.

**65** Lady Margaret Fraser, 1666, by an unknown artist of the Scottish School.
Canvas: 33 × 27 inches (83.8 × 68.5 centimetres).
The Viscount of Arbuthnott.

Widowhood terminated a distinct phase in a woman's life, at once rendering her more vulnerable to external pressures and at the same time giving her greater freedom to choose a partner or an occupation. The change in circumstances brought about by the loss of a husband was visibly emphasised by the mourning garments which many women wore for the rest of their lives. Usually these followed the styles of the time but were made up in black cloth with few trimmings. The covering of the head, however, took the form of an article of clothing worn only for mourning purposes.

These general criteria for mourning costume are seen in the picture of Lady Margaret Fraser during her second widowhood. She lost her first husband, Sir Robert Arbuthnott, in 1633. Finding herself with four sons and three daughters to bring up, she decided to marry again and at the end of the following year became the wife of Sir James Haldane of Gleneagles. An ardent supporter of the Covenant, Sir James was lost at the Battle of Dunbar, leaving Lady Margaret with two more young sons. She did not marry again and when she sat for her portrait fourteen years later she was wearing her mourning garments. On her head is a thick veil over a lace widow's peak. Her dress is the fashion of the period, a dark whisk (cape-like collar) concealing the neckline. The plainness of her attire is somewhat offset by her elaborate jewellery—brooch, necklace, matching bracelets and rings.

**66** Mrs John Livingstone, *c.* 1680, by an unknown artist of the Dutch School, *c.* 1680.
Canvas: $32\frac{1}{2} \times 26\frac{1}{2}$ inches ($82.6 \times 67.3$ centimetres).
The Earl of Wemyss and March KT LLD.

**67** Isabel Preston, Lady Makgill, *c.* 1720, by an unknown artist of the Scottish School.
Canvas: $30 \times 24\frac{1}{2}$ inches ($76.2 \times 62.2$ centimetres).
Colonel R Campbell Preston OBE MC DL.

Muffled in her voluminous mourning garments Mrs Livingstone is the very epitome of widowhood. Cloak, hoods, scarves and a cap with a widow's peak conceal all but her face. Herself the daughter of an Edinburgh merchant she married a Scottish minister who was exiled to Holland and died there. This picture of her in her old age was painted by a Dutch artist so presumably she stayed on in the Low Countries after her husband's death. Her costume is accordingly in the Dutch rather than the Scottish tradition but the next portrait shows that the fashion for all-enveloping mournings was to be found in this country too.

Less overwhelming than the garments of Mrs Livingstone but nonetheless elaborate is the costume of Lady Makgill. She does not wear a dark veil over her head: indeed, the widow's peak familiar in so many earlier pictures was now fast fading in popularity. Instead, women preferred a cap or caps frilled in front and with long ties or lappets left hanging down. Over this, Lady Makgill has a loose-fitting hood, the ends of which are bunched up and tied at intervals with dark cord.

The sitter was the daughter of Sir George Preston of Vallyfield. She married Sir James Makgill of Rankeillor as his second wife and was left a widow in 1699. She did not remarry.

**68** Lady Veronica Bruce, wife of Duncan Campbell
of Kames, *c.* 1723, attributed to Maria Verelst.
Canvas: 36 × 28 inches (91.4 × 71.1 centimetres).
The Earl of Elgin.

A fashion for extreme simplicity in mourning as
in other costume is seen in some portraits of the
1720s, particularly those by Maria Verelst. The
sitter here is wearing almost unrelieved black. On
her head is a plain black veil. Her dress is severely
cut, and completely simple with only the very
edges of the chemise showing at the slit bodice and
sleeves. The low decolletage is uncovered and there
is no longer the feeling that mourning garments
must be voluminous and all-concealing.

Lady Veronica was married twice. A daughter
of the 4th Earl of Kincardine, she first became the
wife of Gustavus Hamilton, a merchant in Edinburgh. On his death she continued his interests in
trade with Boston then in 1703 she remarried. Her
second husband was Duncan Campbell of Kames
and it was after his death that this picture was
painted. As in almost all the female portraits of
the period, no wedding ring is shown.

**69** Janet, Countess of Kincardine, 1767, by J Clarke.
Canvas: 30 × 25 inches (76.2 × 63.5 centimetres).
The Earl of Elgin.

Born Janet Robertson, daughter and heiress of one of the principal clerks of Session, the Countess of Kincardine was left a widow fairly early on in life when her husband died in 1740. She had a young family to bring up and she devoted herself to their interests and to the running of the estates on her son's behalf. In doing so, she paid close and careful attention to every aspect of financial affairs, industrial development, shipping and agriculture. We see her here at about the age of sixty, fashionably dressed in the garments of her day. Probably because she had been a widow for twenty-seven years by the time this picture was painted, she is not dressed in full mourning. The principal evidences of her widowed state are the long, black lace lappets of her cap, carefully arranged across the front of her bodice.

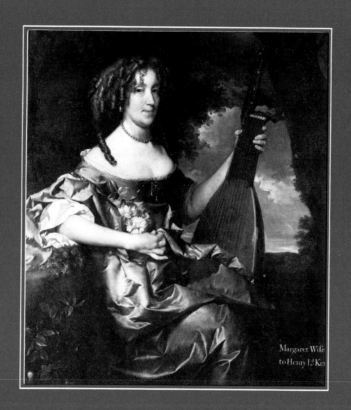

# 6

# Leisure

The women of the seventeenth century did not spend a great deal of time worrying about how best they could occupy their moments of leisure. Taken up as they were with the business of running their households, they had plenty to do. There was as yet no feeling that the simple, domestic tasks of the home were in some way demeaning and the great lady in her castle sewed up shirts for her husband and complained about the price of food just as the other women of the time did. For true recreation, there were various possibilities. Lack of education meant that few women turned to reading to pass the time and those ladies who possessed books owned little other than theological works, supplemented by a few practical manuals on midwifery and cookery. Again, the strictly Presbyterian women, of whom there were many, frowned upon such entertainments as theatres and balls. Not for them the pleasures of the decadent Court in London. Instead, they would engage in sewing, a little music, card games and certain forms of outdoor sport such as falconry and bowling.

By the turn of the century the situation was changing. A lessening of the influence of the Presbyterian ministers combined with an increasing familiarity with more sophisticated London diversions meant that a wider range of activities was becoming acceptable. Indeed, now it was the social pleasures which met with approval, the domestic chores which were scorned. Prejudice against public amusements was dying away. Plays were performed in Edinburgh and the holding of dances culminated in the establishment of the Edinburgh Assembly. The city was becoming a cultural centre in its own right. Ladies spending the winter there took tea together, made up parties to go to the playhouse, held musical evenings and enjoyed gossip, cards and backgammon with the young men who came to call. There were dressmakers to be visited, fashions to be discussed and, with the spread of literacy, novels and romances to be read. Tapestry was laid aside in favour of the new crafts of netting and knotting, newspapers and books of poems were passed round and it gradually came to be that the lady with any social aspirations would abandon all the domestic chores to her servants. For those who could afford thus to delegate their household responsibilities, leisure had become a serious concern and the way in which it was spent a clear indication of status.

**70** Margaret, Lady Ker, *c*. 1672, formerly attributed to Sir Peter Lely.
Canvas: 49½ × 40 inches (125.7 × 101.6 centimetres).
The Duke of Roxburghe.

**71** Letter of Lady Nairne to the Countess of Panmure, 1705.
SRO, Dalhousie Muniments, GD 45/14/245(a).

One woman who by her own account preferred the homely accomplishments to the more sophisticated pleasures offered at Court was Margaret, Lady Nairne. Visiting London in the winter of 1704–5 she took the opportunity of improving a number of her domestic skills, learning amongst other things a new way of making buttons for her husband's shirts.

---

*Nairne February the 5th*
*1705.*

*Last time I writt to Your Ladyship I forgot to*
*tell you that I think I've now found out the*
*true way of making the thread buttons. I*
*send a couple inclos'd. The way of doing 'em*
*is not with thread befor the needle except the first row*
*but puting*
*it so        through the stitch to the left*
*hand. If this discription be not intilegible,*
*I shall endevour to make it plainer in my next.*
*The want of moulds at Dunkel[d] and the reading*
*in the votes of the English Parliament about the*
*bean and berry button makers put me upon*
*my invention to find out what was meant*
*by it. I now make the moulds of the half of*
*a pea, which I either make myself or gets*
*some of the idle men to do it for me and so saves*
*the trouble of having moulds from wrights.*
*One of those inclosed has a pea mould and I*
*send Your Ladyship two without covers that if you*
*like the contrivance, you may see by that*
*how 'tis done. The pea this button was made*
*of is too little, but that Your Ladyship knows I think*
*no fault for My Lord's hand wrists [ie ruffles] . . .*

**72** Matilda Lockhart-Wishart, *c.* 1768, attributed to George Knapton.
Canvas: 36 × 28 inches (91.4 × 71.1 centimetres).
A H Macdonald Lockhart Esq.

No self-respecting lady would have had her portrait painted while she was busily making shirt buttons, but the elegant craft of knotting was a different matter. It involved the use of an ornamental shuttle, often inlaid with precious metal, a reel of thread and a decorative bag in which these materials could be kept. It was a graceful occupation which looked well when done in public and the little bag could easily be carried about with its owner. At first sight the shuttle resembles the kind used for tatting, but in fact it is larger and is open at each end which a tatting shuttle is not. Matilda would be making a trimming for either a garment or for some item of furnishing, because in knotting a plain length of yarn was decorated with knots or picots.

[Information from Mrs Helen Bennett, National Museum of Antiquities of Scotland: see also Sylvia Graves, *The History of Needlework Tools and Accessories* (1973), 85–8.]

**73** Lady Elizabeth Leslie, Countess of Hopetoun, *c.* 1767, by Thomas Gainsborough.
Canvas: 50 × 40 inches (127 × 101.6 centimetres).
In a Scottish Private Collection.

**74** Lady Caroline Hunter, *c.* 1760, attributed to William Millar.
Canvas: 30 × 25 inches (76.2 × 63.5 centimetres).
The Lord Forbes KBE.

Another new form of craft which became popular in the mid-eighteenth century was tambouring. This type of embroidery originated in the Orient and was brought back to France in about 1750, where it immediately interested ladies as a means of decorating muslin. In an early painting by Gainsborough, Lady Elizabeth Leslie, Countess of Hopetoun sits at her tambour frame, hook in hand. She works a continuous chain stitch on her fabric, which is stretched tightly across the frame. The tambour hook was similar to a metal crochet hook although sharper and with a broader handle to give the fingers a firm grip. The Countess holds her hook vertically, ready to insert it downwards through the material, producing a series of loops, each tethered by the one before.

A chain stitch could be produced much more quickly with the tambour hook than with the needle. The continuous threads needed for the work can be seen coming from the reel which is fixed underneath the frame.

[Information from Mrs Helen Bennett, National Museum of Antiquities of Scotland: see also Margaret H Swain, *The Flowerers* (Edinburgh 1955).]

Rather less exotic than tambouring but much in favour was the long-established pastime of knitting. The portrait of Lady Caroline Hunter is particularly charming because it records in faithful detail a skill normally judged too mundane to be included in a portrait. It is thus appropriate that the sitter wears her morning or everyday garments rather than her best clothes. She has chosen to be seen as her family and friends saw her rather than as a lady of fashion in society. Even so, she could reassure herself with the thought that knitting, if dull, was a perfectly suitable occupation for an Earl's daughter. In 1733 it had been proudly noted that the Duke of Perth's daughter Lady Mary Drummond 'had spun from Scottish wool three pairs of knitted gloves or mitts, which were estimated at three guineas each pair.'

The technique of knitting shown in Lady Caroline's picture is in itself interesting for it demonstrates a method which was at one time widely practised. The knitter is using a sheath of quills or straw which is pinned to the front of her bodice. This supports the needle, thereby allowing her fingers to move to and fro near its top so that

she could make much quicker progress. In Shetland the knitting belt serves this purpose. The knitting itself—a stocking or perhaps a long nightcap—is tucked under Lady Caroline's left arm and may have been pinned to the back of her bodice, another way of increasing speed.

[Information from Mrs Helen Bennett, National Museum of Antiquities of Scotland: quotation from *Kennedy's Annals of Aberdeen* (London 1818) ii, 197].

**75** Lady Elizabeth Carnegie, Countess of Hopetoun, *c.* 1780, by David Allan.
Canvas: 36 × 28 inches (91.4 × 71.1 centimetres).
In a Scottish Private Collection.

Apart from what may be termed handicrafts, another necessary accomplishment for the fashionable young lady of the eighteenth century was the ability to sketch. Taught by a drawing master when she was in her teens, she would continue to produce landscapes and sometimes portraits for her own amusement and for the entertainment of her family and friends. Dame Janet Dick of Prestonfield, for example, was in the habit of diverting some of her correspondents by including in her letters little pictures she had drawn of local activities. The lady seated here proudly holding her landscape is Elizabeth Carnegie, eldest daughter of George, 6th Earl of Northesk. When she was only sixteen she married the Earl of Hopetoun and had by him six daughters before her death in 1793 at the age of forty-three.

**76** Frances Pierrepoint, Countess of Mar, 1714–15,
by Sir Godfrey Kneller.
Canvas: 93½ × 58 inches (217.2 × 147.4 centimetres).
The Earl of Mar and Kellie: on loan to the Scottish
National Portrait Gallery.

Restricted as they were by the difficulties of travel, many women must have regarded riding as a necessity rather than a recreation. As a mode of transport it was quicker and more comfortable than making a journey by sedan chair or by coach and Anne, 3rd Duchess of Hamilton, for example, still rode quite long distances when she was in her sixties. In common with her contemporaries, she did enjoy the outdoor exercise it afforded her as well as appreciating its other advantages.

Women rode side-saddle, of course, on their own horse if they had one or behind their husband on his if they did not. Aristocratic ladies possessed a special riding habit like the splendid outfit worn by the Earl of Mar's second wife when her portrait was painted by Kneller. Her costume has a distinctly masculine air about it. Her jacket is cut like a man's coat and round her neck she has a Steinkirk cravat. Beneath the coat is a matching waistcoat, possibly a false one consisting of front panels sewn to the lining of the coat at either side. Under her arm is a tricorne hat, again a masculine fashion, and on her head is a long, curly wig. Her petticoat has a deep, inverted flounce and is deceptive in appearance. It would be not a full skirt but an apron-like garment with riding breeches of some kind worn beneath. The outfit is made up in a soft, pink material, the masculine features of coat and cravat serving only to enhance the femininity of the total effect.

[See C Willett and Phillis Cunnington, *Handbook of English Costume in the Eighteenth Century* (London 1957), 134–5.]

Part of feminine leisure was of course devoted to the appearance. Women wanted to look their best when they appeared in public and so they ordered the most fashionable dresses they could afford, dressed their hair in the latest style and purchased powder, patches and various lotions. The range of cosmetics was relatively small, but many women possessed recipes for well-tried concoctions. Lady Orbiston's name, for example, appears on this recipe for cosmetic lotion which she probably sent to her friend Margaret, Countess of Panmure.

**77** A Recipe for Cosmetic Lotion, *c.* 1720.
SRO, Dalhousie Muniments, GD 45/26/150.

*Take of barley and rosewater of each*
*halfe a mutchken, bitter almonds two unces.*
*Blanch and beat them well in a marble mortar*
*then add the waters by degrees till well*
*incorporate. Strain through an hair search [sieve]*
*and to the liquor add two drahms of camphire*
*dissolved in spirit of wine or Hungary Water.*
*It may be us[e]d without the*
*camphire sometimes.*
*Lady Orbiston*

A fan was not only an indispensible accessory for the lady of fashion, but it could be a subtle means of expressing its owner's political sympathies. This example is traditionally said to have been designed and engraved by Sir Robert Strange for the ladies of Prince Charles Edward's Court in Edinburgh in 1745. Its handpainted leaf shows the Prince in armour surrounded by all manner of allegorical figures and devices including Venus, Cupid and Fame, Prince Charles Edward himself, flaming hearts, a dove with an olive branch—and George II and his family in retreat on the right.

**78** Fan designed by Sir Robert Strange.
National Museum of Antiquities of Scotland, UI 3.

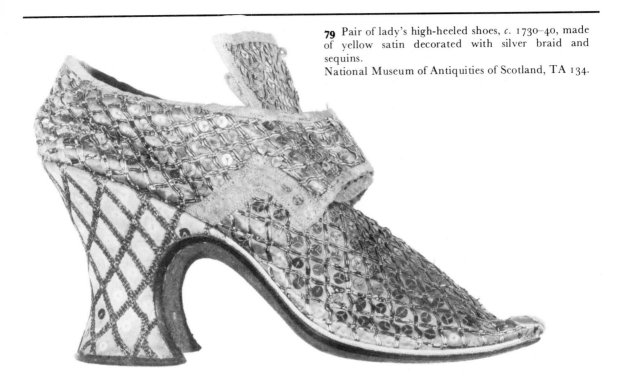

**79** Pair of lady's high-heeled shoes, *c.* 1730–40, made of yellow satin decorated with silver braid and sequins.
National Museum of Antiquities of Scotland, TA 134.

Towards the end of the seventeenth century public balls were becoming increasingly popular and royal approval for this form of entertainment came in 1703 when Queen Anne paid a visit to Bath. An 'assembly' for card playing and dancing was held in her presence and so popular did it prove that 'assemblies' spread rapidly throughout the country. About 1710 a house at the West Bow in Edinburgh was put to this use but it was not until 1723 that the Edinburgh Assembly proper was established in a large hall in what was later to be named Old Assembly Close, off the High Street.

One lady who viewed its opening with scant enthusiasm was Margaret, Countess of Panmure. Amusing her exiled husband as usual with letters full of the latest news, she wrote on 24 January 1723 to tell him, 'There are not many comppany here this winter, but we have gott a new diversion here which is an Assemblie, which I believe will take very well in spight of the Presbyterian ministers' railing att it. I have been att one of the young folks' dances and the elder ones lookes one [ie on]. They are to play att litle games, I mean for litle money but I am to be no gamester and I believe shall go but seldom. The President of the [Court of] Session I am told was there this night to be an incouridgment to it, so att last you may imagin Old Reeky will grow polit with the rest of the world. I wish you were here to see it.'

In fact card games were abandoned early on and the Edinburgh Assembly was strictly run with great decorum by a number of well known aristocratic ladies, the leader of whom was soon to be none other than the Countess of Panmure.

Each Thursday at 4 pm the ladies and gentlemen of the city hurried to the Hall with their half crown tickets, ready to enjoy the entertainment. At a signal from the presiding Lady Directoress, dancing began. There were minuets until the interval, when tea, coffee, chocolate and biscuits were available. Country dancing continued until 11 pm. All the proceeds went to charity, hence the involvement of the Lady Directoresses and even in the face of the energetic opposition of the ministers the Assembly proved a great success. In spite of the rigid formality of its proceedings, a feature often noted by English visitors, it provided new opportunities for young people to meet each other and to find entirely respectable marriage partners in surroundings outwith their own homes. Limited this freedom might be, but it had been unknown a hundred years earlier.

[James H Jamieson, 'Social Assemblies of the Eighteenth Century' in *The Book of the Old Edinburgh Club*, xix (1933), 51: quotation from SRO, Dalhousie Muniments, GD 45/14/220/145.]

**80** Badge of the Lady Directoress of the Edinburgh Assembly, 1724.
National Museum of Antiquities of Scotland, M 37.

# ADVERTISEMENT

By Order of the Right Honourable,

MARGARET Countess of *Panmure*, HENRIETTA HAMILTON Lady *Orbeston*, ELISABETH HAMILTON Lady *Northberwick*, and KATHARINE JOHNSTON Lady *Newhall*,

DIRECTORS of the

# EDINBURGH ASSEMBLY,

*For the Encouragement of the Manufactories of this Country.*

WHEREAS the Trustees for the Manufactories, and the SOCIETY for Agriculture, have signified to us the LADIES who have the Honour of the Government and Direction of this ASSEMBLY, That it will contribute very much for the Encouragement of all Sorts of Manufactories, and tend to promote a Spirit of Virtue and Industry in Persons of all Ranks, if the Ladies and Gentlemen who frequent this ASSEMBLY, would be perswaded to appear here once or twice in the Year at least, dressed in the Manufacture of this Country: And if at all Times, no other Linen nor Lace should be worn in this ASSEMBLY, but what is manufactured in *GREAT BRITAIN*.

WE therefore, the said LADIES, most heartily agreeing with the said Trustees and Society, do hereby seriously recommend to all LADIES and GENTLEMEN, who are pleased to come to this ASSEMBLY, that they would appear here, on the last *Thursday* of *July* next; and on the last *Thursday* of *January* and *July* every Year hereafter, dressed in the Manufacture of this Country: And that at all Times thereafter, no Linen or Lace be worn in this ASSEMBLY, but what shall be made in *GREAT BRITAIN*.

WHICH Request of ours, is not understood to be addressed to any who have not their Residence in *SCOTLAND*.

THE Compliance of the LADIES and GENTLEMEN to this Appointment, tending so visibly to the GOOD of this Country, will be very satisfying to the said Trustees and Society, and most agreeable to us the said LADIES, who will thereby be encouraged in our Government and Direction, and with greater Pleasure attend the ASSEMBLY.

*Given at the Assembly-Hall, this Fifteenth Day of* February, *One thousand seven hundred and twenty eight, and subscribed by*

MARGARET PANMURE.
HENRIETTA HAMILTON.
ELISABETH HAMILTON.
KATHARINE JOHNSTON.

**81** Advertisement by the Edinburgh Assembly asking that garments made of British linen and lace should be worn at twice-yearly meetings, 1728. SRO, Dalhousie Muniments, GD 45/24/79.

**82** Rules of the Edinburgh Assembly, 1746.
(To be hung up in the lobby of the Hall)

DATE DUE

*No lady to be admitted in a nightgown [ie a dressing gown] and no gentleman in boots.*
*Dancing to begin precisely at 5 o'clock afternoon in the winter and at 6 in summer.*
*Each set not to exceed ten couples to dance but one country dance at a time.*
*The couples to dance their minuets in the order they stand in their several sets.*
*No dancing out of the regular order but by leave from the Lady Directress of the night.*
*No dancing whatever to be allowed but in the ordinary dancing place.*
*No dance to begin after 11 at night.*
*No misses in skirts and jackets, robecoats nor*
*staybodied gowns to be allowed to dance*
*country dances but in a set by themselves.*
*No tea, coffee, negus nor other liquor to be carried*
*into the dancing room.*
*It is expected no gentleman will step over the*
*rail round the dancing place but will enter or go*
*out by the doors at the upper or lower end of the*
*room and that all ladys and gentlemen*
*will order their servants not to enter the passage*
*before the outer door with lighted flambeaux.*

[Minute Book of the Edinburgh Assembly, 1746: printed in James H Jamieson, 'Social Assemblies of the Eighteenth Century' in *The Book of the Old Edinburgh Club*, xix (1933), 51.]

Printed in Scotland for H.M.S.O. by Alna Press Ltd., D'd 587800/6028 5/79.